Imago Christi, A Horizon of Human Becoming

Christian Heritage Rediscovered

The Series, as the name suggests, is meant to focus on Christian Faith & Living vis-à-vis topics like Literature & Poetry, Indigenous Philosophizing, Ethical response towards Agriculture, Health & Healing, Science & Technology, Eco-feminist Theology, Sociological approach towards Human Rights, Law & Politics, Arts, History of Ideas, Ancient Civilizations, Cultural Contiguity, Religious Cosmologies & Mysticism, Footsteps of famous Theologians, World Peace & Harmony, Global Capitalism, Network Marketing, Cybertheology, Population & Demographics, Epigraphic Studies, Contextualized Education, and many others. We welcome a Mss. on any topic/s mentioned, whether they are original works, scholarly monographs, collections of conference papers, revised dissertations, or translations of historical documents. Through the Series we, the Publishers, are striving to put forward published works that may help Institutions, Academic Bodies, Researchers, Scholars and the World at large in furthering their respective knowledge and understanding on the concerned subject. We welcome your comments on our efforts and further suggestions on how we can foster the upcoming thought provoking theologically grounded books.

Christian Heritage Rediscovered - 59

Imago Christi, A Horizon of Human Becoming

Christology Engaged in Cross-Cultural Theological Anthropology

Johny C. Lalhmingmawia

CWI

Christian World Imprints™

First Published in 2018 by

Christian World Imprints™
Christian Publishing & Books from India
H-12 Bali Nagar, **New Delhi-110015**
info@christianworldimprints.com
www.ChristianWorldImprints.com
Phone: +91 11 25465925

ISBN: 978-93-5148-246-8 (HB) ISBN: 978-93-5148-247-5 (PB)

Cataloging in Publication Data--DK
Courtesy: D.K. Agencies (P) Ltd. <docinfo@dkagencies.com>

Lalhmingmawia, Johny C., author.
Imago Christi, a horizon of human becoming : Christology engaged in cross-cultural theological anthropology / Johny C. Lalhmingmawia.
pages cm. -- (Christian heritage rediscovered ; 59)
Includes bibliographical references.
ISBN 9789351482468 (HB)
ISBN 9789351482475 (PB)

1. Theological anthropology--Christianity. 2. Theological anthropology--Cross-cultural studies. 3. Schleiermacher, Friedrich, 1768-1834. 4. Panikkar, Raimon, 1918-2010. I. Title. II. Series: Christian heritage rediscovered ; 59.

LCC BT701.3.L35 2017 | DDC 233.5 23

Printed in India.

Dedication

This humble work is dedicated to my late grand-father Upa C. Lalduha (1933-2017), who was the very source of inspiration in my life. The life that he lived left me abundant lessons that I should hold on. I deeply treasure his advices, encouragements and most of all his prayer was the source of my strength.

This book in its original form is the thesis submitted to the Senate of Serampore College (University), India, towards the degree of Master of Theology and is published with the written permission. The author is responsible for the title, contents and opinions in it.

The original title of the thesis is "An Exploration of 'Perfection and Blessedness' in the Christology of Friedrich Schleiermacher and 'Fullness of Man' in the Christophany of Raimond Panikkar for a Cross-Cultural Theological Anthropology."

Contents

Foreword

In *Imago Christi, A Horizon of Human Becoming,* Johny C. Lalhmingmawia flips the *imago Dei*-inflected understandings of humanity to explore *imago Christi* as an analytical frame for theological anthropology. Wading through a wide spectrum of theological resources, Johny's exploration hones in on focused readings of Friedrich Schleiermacher and Raimundo Panikkar both for the intricacies of their ideas and for the intercultural variety they represent. It would benefit the reader to pay close attention to Johny's prose as he meticulously builds his case for the Christological foundations of theological anthropology. Such an exploration is neither the first nor the last of its kind. However, Johny lays down a template robust enough that any further development will have to reckon with the argumentation in *Imago Christi.*

Dr. Lalruatkima
AICS, Aizawl

Acknowledgement

The completion of this work calls for acknowledging some persons from whom invaluable help and earnest support I received. I give thanks to the Almighty God, who is the source of my being and my guide, who provides an ever help and sustenance of all my needs. My heartfelt thanks go to the Baptist Church of Mizoram from where I have been receiving support and scholarship that enables me to take my theological journey thus far.

I am deeply indebted to my mentor, Rev. Dr. Joseph Prabhakar Dyam, for his valuable encouragement and sensible advice. It was indeed from him that motivation for pursuing the completion of this work was facilitated. His companionship was memorable.

I am exceedingly grateful to Dr. Lalruatkima who sincerely looked through and did editing for the improvement of the work. Not only that, but engaged himself with the issue taken up in the work and opened my eyes to see some probable loopholes to keep me pressing on to further pursuit.

I am genuinely grateful to my beloved family who gave me unfailing support for my studies and the ministry that I am pursuing. Joy is abundant with love and unfailing support from my beloved wife Tetei Fanai, with whom we could make out this journey of life a charming one.

Acknowledgements

[illegible]

Introduction

As Christian theology envisions *Imago Christi* to be the horizon of human becoming, a Christian anthropology needs to be grounded in Christology. This book argues that Christology is pivotal for an intercultural reading of the human and divine relationship. Bringing up to speed the insights from Friedrich Schleiermacher's understanding of "Perfection and Blessedness" and Raimond Panikkar's understanding of the "Fullness of Man," the argument envisions a theological anthropology consonant with contemporary cross-cultural issues.

Schleiermacher explains that Jesus Christ is ordained to be the person through whom the whole human race is to be completed and perfected.[1] Having a living fellowship with the Redeemer is having fellowship with God, which is to share the 'perfection and blessedness of Christ.' In Schleiermacher's understanding, 'perfection' is similar to the completion of creation. Christ is the Second Adam who is the beginner and originator of perfect human life. Christ is like other human beings, descended from the first Adam, who has absolutely potent God-consciousness. Though Christ does not belong to the former order, but placed in the historical order and stands under the law of historical development in His whole activity which is brought to perfection through gradual expansion, from the point at which He appears.[2]

---

[1] Friedrich Schleiermacher, *The Christian Faith,* edited by H. R. Mackintosh and J. S. Stewart (Edinburgh: T & T Clark, 1928), p. 368.

[2] Schleiermacher, *The Christian Faith* ..., p. 367.

Panikkar talks about the 'Fullness of Man' in his discussion on the Christophany[3] that "In Jesus Christ the finite and the infinite meet, the human and the divine are joined. In him the material and the spiritual are one, and also the male and the female, high and low, heaven and earth, the historical and the transhistorical, time and eternity."[4] Panikkar's Christophany intends to offer an image of Christ that all people are capable of believing in and to offer the same experience to all those who nourish an interest in the person, Jesus.[5]

Theological anthropology is a study of the human person in relation to a divine being. Christian theology addresses human being as created in the Image of God and Christ as the true human being. Therefore, this book will locate a cross-cultural theological anthropology at the intersection of Friedrich Schleiermacher's idea of "Perfection and Blessedness" and Raimond Panikkar's musings on the "Fulness of Man."

This is an attempt to pursue the understanding of humanity, in the conceptual level, grounded in the Christian understanding of Christ. Selecting Schleiermacher and Panikkar, is an intention to engage in a cross-cultural interaction with a concern to bring out better understanding of humanity for our time. The study will engaged in Christology with a hope to offer an image of Christ that the modern contemporary people are capable of believing in, so as to strengthen the life of each and every individual of a community.

Theological anthropology has always been a very important area of study and several researches have been done on Christian understanding of anthropology. However, this study attempts to look at the human horizon in a cross-cultural context, in which area there is a lack of in-depth study. In regard to both, Schleiermacher and Panikkar, most writings are mainly descriptive and in the form

---

[3] Panikkar uses the term a 'Christophany,' to mean a manifestation of Christ to human consciousness which includes an experience of Christ as well as a critical reflection on that experience. He says that "Christophany is the Symbol of the *Mysterium conjunctionis* of Divine, Human, and Cosmic Reality." See Raimon Panikkar, *The Fulness of Man: A Christophany,* translated by Alfred DiLascia (New York: Orbis Books and Delhi: ISPCK, 2006), p. 181.

[4] Panikkar, *The Fulness of Man* ..., p. 181.

[5] Panikkar, *The Fulness of Man* ..., p. 9.

of commentary. There is no clear focus on theological anthropology as such. In *The Cambridge Companion to Friedrich Schleiermacher* (2005), Jacqueline Marina's essay on the topic of "Christology and Anthropology in Friedrich Schleiermacher," limits the discussion of anthropology to a description of the person and work of Christ in Schleiermacher's thought. In the case of Panikkar, he, himself, interacting cross culturally is evidence that his theological formulation seriously takes up the issue of humanity.

Therefore, making use of the primary resources with the help of secondary materials, this study will venture the understanding of humanity in their theology seeking resources for constructing theological anthropology.

In the first chapter, there will be an explanation on theological anthropology and the need for cross cultural interaction in theological anthropology. We will discuss human subjectivity in doing theology followed by the relation of theology and anthropology. After that we will have a discussion on the mystery of human being followed by our discussion on human dignity in relation to image of God. Then, we will bring our proposal to have image of Christ as the key to understand human identity.

In the second chapter, there will be an exploration of Schleiermacher's personal cultural background, his life, work and his thought that reflect his methodological undertaking. We will have a description of his understanding of religion and Christ. Then, we will make our proposal to have a Christological foundation for understanding humanity. Reflecting upon our discussion on Schleieramcher, we will bring our insights for the understanding of human being with a critical assessment on Schleiermacher.

In the third chapter, we will have an exploration of Panikkar's personal cross-cultural background, his life, work and his methodological undertaking. We will explore his understanding of Christ as Reality, who is the source and end of all beings. There will be a discussion on his proposal of christophany for the expansion of traditional understanding of Christology. Then, we will bring our insights we get from our discussion on Panikkar followed by a critical reflection on Panikkar's understanding of divinization.

In the fourth chapter, we will deal with Christological issues that involved in constructing cross-cultural theological anthropology. We will discuss image of Christ in creation and incarnation followed by our quest of humanity in the image of Christ through understanding Christ as true human being, origin and destiny of human being. We will, then, formulate the understanding of humanity through the insights that we get from our cross-cultural theological interaction.

In the fifth chapter, the research will be concluded with a brief summary of each chapter and reflection on humanity in the light of cross-cultural interaction.

Chapter 1

Image of God as Image of Christ A New Horizon in Theological Anthropology

1.1. Introduction:

Changing human conditions and histories engender new questions about the change and its effects. Theology always needs reinterpretation, reevaluation and reformulation in order to be meaningful. One of the important characteristics of Christian theology is that it is dynamic, not static ideology, for it always seeks new horizons with the changing situation. Due to the ambiguities of human nature, there are various understandings and approaches to the question of humanity. One possible way of looking at theology is that it is a search for true humanity in the light of the transcendental being, or God. However, theology is not purely a transcendental activity, it is engaged in the life, history and struggles of the people. Today, with the consciousness of the validity of human experience as the source, theology becomes people oriented.

Theological anthropology has been traditionally grounded in the image of God. To shift from this position, we will base theological anthropology on the image of Christ, which seeks a new horizon by affirming human dimension in the image of Christ. As we are making a move from the image of God to image of Christ for the foundation of theological anthropology, this shift to Christology will in turn facilitate the cross-cultural interaction.

1.2. Meaning and Origin of Theological Anthropology:

To begin our discussion on theological anthropology, we will briefly look at the meaning, origin and development of the term 'theological anthropology.'

1.2.1. Meaning: *The Cambridge Dictionary of Christian Theology* (2011) says that 'theological anthropology' refers to the Christian doctrine of human being, which methodologically differs from social-scientific disciplines like cultural, physical, or social anthropology for it is specifically concerned with humanity's relationship to the triune God. It is a sub-topic of the 'Doctrine of Creation' for human being is understood as being made by God like all other entities. There is a close relation to Christology for the Second Person of the Trinity, Jesus of Nazareth, who lived a human life, is central to Christian Faith.[1] The *Encyclopedia of Christianity* (2005) says that theological anthropology is a systematic reflection on human nature and destiny in the light of the biblical witness. It does not simply challenge various anthropological sciences. However, insofar as these sciences say true things about humanity, theological anthropology accepts them as thematic enrichment, warning, and delimitation.[2]

Reinhold Niebuhr uses two words "Nature and Destiny"[3] together in his anthropological groundwork. This clearly reflects that the ground and true dignity of human being as well as the vocation and providence of human being are the anthropological enterprise. Therefore, 'Theological Anthropology,' to put it shortly, is the study of the human person in relation to a divine being.

---

[1] Ian A. McFarland, "Theological Anthropology," in *The Cambridge Dictionary of Christian Theology*, edited by Ian A. McFarland, et al. (New York: Cambridge University Press, 2011), p. 501.

[2] Dietrich Ritschl, "Anthropology," in *Encyclopedia of Christianity*, edited by Erwin Fahlbusch, et al., vol. I (A – B) (Brill: William B. Eerdmans Publishing Company, 1999), p. 69.

[3] Reinhold Niebuhr published his book "Human Nature and Destiny of Man: A Christian Interpretation" in the year 1941 and 1943.

1.2.2. Origin and Development: Dietrich Ritschl says that we find no theological anthropology as such in the Church history. However, the church developed a series of related individual themes deriving from both biblical tradition and ancient philosophy. The classical theology was dominated by the question of human soul.[4] As Heimo Hofmeister says, the attempt to define human nature occurred within the context of a total interpretation of being (ontology) until the modern period. The construction of anthropology as an independent discipline began with the criticism of the metaphysical tradition and attempt to find a new basis for philosophy.[5]

Pannenberg says that the development of understanding human being as the foundation of modern theology can be traced in Protestant theology through various stages. Through Deism and the moral rationalism of the later Enlightenment, it started from the early bias toward a "praxis" springing from the human need of redemption. Then, into the classical period of German evangelical theology that began with Schleiermacher's definition of religion. It continued through the revivalist theology and succeeded by liberal theology. Debates occasioned by dialectical theology culminated in an existentialist interpretation of the Christian message from Rudolf Bultmann, in opposition to Karl Barth. After the holding action of the neo-Scholastic revival, Catholic theology has finally run the same course, as we see in the theology of Karl Rahner.[6] However, the development of modern philosophy was one of the stimuli for the growing anthropocentrism of modern theology, but not due solely to the influence of philosophy. In fact, the foundation for Christian theological concentration on the human person was already laid in the early Christian faith in the incarnation of God.[7]

---

[4] Ritschl, "Anthropology," in *Encyclopedia of Christianity* ..., p. 74.

[5] Heimo Hofmeister, "Philosophical Anthropology," in *Encyclopedia of Christianity* ..., p. 75.

[6] Wolfhart Pannenberg, *Anthropology in Theological Perspective* (Edinburgh: T & T Clark Ltd, 1985), p. 11.

[7] Pannenberg, *Anthropology in Theological* ..., p. 12.

1.3. Theological Anthropology for Our Time:

David H. Kelsey deals with the systematic formulation of theological anthropology in his *Eccentric Existence* (2009). He asserts that the Christian faith has nonnegotiable claims about human beings, namely "(a) God actively relates to human beings to create them, (b) to draw them to eschatological consummation, and (c) to reconcile them when they are alienated from God." Additionally, there are three correlative perennial anthropological questions, such as "what are we?" "who are we?" and "How we ought to be?" these should be reframed in ways shaped by Christian background beliefs about our ultimate and proximate contexts.[8] So, his main hypothesis is that, in the current primary theology, there are reasons to reexamine the adequacy of received theological anthropological formulations. Therefore, the intersection of the claims about human beings the three perennial anthropological questions generate a structure for *Eccentric Existence.*[9]

However, the Faith and Order Commission of the World Council of Churches, which made a study on Theological Anthropology, explores contemporary challenges to the traditional understanding of humanity as "made in the image of God." The Faith and Order Paper no. 199 (2005), "Christian Perspectives on Theological Anthropology," was not intended to develop a comprehensive systematic Christian anthropology. It rather seeks to reflect on complex and sensitive issues related to a Christian understanding of human nature paying close attention to challenges which face humanity today.[10] This shows that theology, today, trains its focus onhumanity as the contemporary situation requires.

However, the systematic formulation of theology is always important and cannot be neglected. We, therefore, need to formulate a theological anthropology, which is systematic and that would respond to the contemporary challenges. This is not to formulate

[8] David H. Kelsey, *Eccentric Existence: A Theological Anthropology,* vol. 1 (Louisville, Kentucky: Westminster John Knox Press, 2009), p. 8.

[9] Kelsey, *Eccentric Existence* ..., p. 10.

[10] "Christian Perspectives on Theological Anthropology," http://www.oikoumene.org/fileadmin/files/wcc-main/documents/p2/FO2005, 199, en.pdf. p. 1. (Accessed on 5th October, 2012).

a universal theology but a theology upon which reflection could be done from various contexts in relation to the issues and challenges of our time.

1.4. Cross-Cultural Theological Anthropology: A Contemporary Challenge:

While Christian theology always claims universality, it is important to question what true Catholicity is. Kuncheria Pathil says that Christian theology today, if it claims to be catholic, also needs to be inter-cultural. It needs to be relevant and ultimately meaningful also for other cultures. Each culture, being a universe of its own, runs the danger of stagnation if it is not ready to be fecundated by other cultures. Each culture has its own understanding and interpretation of the ultimate mystery of reality and the meaning of life, but uses different languages.[11]

Volker Kuster argues for the necessity of intercultural theology in a pluralistic context in order to dialogue with different discourses. He says that "Christian faith lives from the multiplicity of strands of traditions which preserve its richness, open up different perspectives on the truth and, ideally, mutually correct one another."[12] M. Thomas Thangaraj says that the European (the West) theology has been normative for all theological reflection and construction. Today, this false sense of universalism has been challenged by the shift in emphasis to contextualization. He says that contextualization, as a reaction against a domineering and subjugating type of universalizing, "was a way of joining the global discussion without allowing oneself to be dominated by theologies in the West."[13] He argues that the local-global interaction is possible through Christology for "Christology has always been an exercise in dialogue."[14]

---

[11] Kuncheria Pathil and Mathew Paikada, eds., *Indian Theology Seeking New Horizons* (Mumbai: St. Pauls, 2007), p. 132.

[12] Volker Kuster, *The Many Faces of Jesus Christ* (Maryknoll, New York: Orbis Books, 2001), p. 35.

[13] M. Thomas Thangaraj, *The Crucified Guru* (Nashville: Abingdon Press, 1994), p. 21.

[14] Thangaraj, *The Crucified Guru* ..., p. 24.

Taking this stance that Christology itself is an engagement in cross-cultural interaction, we attempt to develop a cross-cultural theological anthropology on the grounds of Christology (*imago Christi* not *imago Dei*). In this cross-cultural interaction, we have the affirmation that Christology is the very foundation of a dynamic relation between transcendent and immanent, divine and human, universal and contextual. Understanding cultures in terms of two Christological traditions, such as: the divinity and humanity, we are trying to bring out the dynamic relation of the binaries to combat the polarization of opposite traditions. With this cross-cultural interaction of two traditions, our understanding of humanity would be more catholic and contextual to have an authentic life and better humanity.

1.5. Human Being as the Subject Matter of Theology:

Pannenberg says that the understanding of the human being has increasingly played a foundational role in the history of modern theology.[15] James Luther Mays says that the Bible is about God and human being. From Genesis to Revelation, Both God and humankind are the subjects. Each book of the scripture tells about God's way with human beings, their life in the world, and can be read as a vast theological anthropology. "Any of its texts can serve as a source for reflection on the human identity and condition."[16]

Theology today is not just faith seeking understanding, it has turned towards human science and becomes people's theology for the transformation of human and the world. The so called 'Contextual theology' has been developed with the new consciousness of the importance of human dignity and identity. Kuncheria Pathil says that theology, today, has developed new horizons as the faith experience of a contemporary Christian community becomes the source of new theologies.[17] Theology, then, tends towards anthropology and become relevant and meaningful only when its formulation is connected to

---

[15] Pannenberg, *Anthropology in Theological* ..., p. 11.

[16] James Luther Mays, "The Self in the Psalms and the Image of God," in *God and Human Dignity*, edited by R. Kendall Soulen and Linda Woodhead (Grand Rapids: William B. Eerdmans Publishing Company, 2006), p. 27.

[17] Pathil, *Indian Theology Seeking* ..., p. 54.

our own human self-understanding in the light of our experience. This concept of theology challenges the traditional understanding of theology both in the Western and the Eastern context. Therefore, theology should have its focus on humanity and should be based on the community's experience of today.[18]

1.6. The Relation of Theology and Anthropology:

While anthropology is concerned with an understanding of human experience, theology is concerned with God. Charles Cameron, then, asks what lies behind the idea of producing a theological anthropology and the importance of having a distinctive theological anthropology. He says that there is a real need to take a theological point of view towards anthropology to understand human experience. This concerns a better understanding of ourselves which cannot be left by theologians to others.[19] However, there could be certain approaches, with different methodological postures of theologians, towards the relation between theology and anthropology.

1.6.1. Immanental Approach: Friedrich Schleiermacher attempted to reconstruct Christian doctrine basing theology on 'human experience.'[20] This involves the understanding of religion as rooted in and even identical with an experience essential to true humanity.[21] His attempt, coming in the aftermath of enlightenment, is set alongside of both the Kantian knowledge of God on practical reason and Hegelian new speculative rationalism that detects the march of Absolute Spirit through history. Providing an alternative approach, Schleiermacher sought, based on 'intuition,' a fundamental universal human feeling of dependence on the whole of reality.[22]

---

[18] Pathil, *Indian Theology Seeking ...*, p. 57.

[19] Charles Cameron, "An Introduction to 'Theological Anthropology'," *Evangel*, 23.2 (Summer, 2005): p. 53.

[20] Schleiermacher developed "feeling" as the ground of religion. It will be dealt, in detail, in Chapter Two.

[21] Keith W. Clements, *Friedrich Schleiermacher, Pioneer of Modern Theology* (London and San Francisco: Collins, 1987), p. 11.

[22] Stanley J. Grenz and Roger E. Olson, *20th Century Theology* (Secunderabad: OM Authentic Books, 1992), p. 43.

In the twentieth century, however, Schleiermacher's methodological groundwork has been detracted by Karl Barth and accused him of speaking about God by speaking about human being. Barth charged him as radically anthropocentric which set the course of the proclamation of God to be dead in the mid-twentieth century by certain theologians.[23] Barth says that there is no revelation reflected neither in dogma nor in the refraction of the subject matter of dogmatics. But Christian faith is reflected in the basic tenets of a particular church (evangelical) not in dogmatics.[24]

1.6.2. Transcendental Approach: Karl Barth, having revelation of God as his epistemological foundation, argues for the Word of God as the source of our knowledge of the nature of human being as created by God. Human being living under heaven and on earth is the creature who is related to God.[25] He says that "the knowledge of man (sic) is possible and attainable only from the standpoint of the knowledge of God."[26] David Cairns says that there is no more fundamental debate in the world today than that about the nature of human being. Politicians, economists, philosophers and scientists all have their views of human nature, and a Christian believer cannot withdraw oneself from this debate. The interest of various rivals of Christianity in the debate is more and more being moved away from the sphere of God to the question of human being. However, Cairns' conviction is that the whole doctrine of human being is faulty without understanding the human essential dependence and relationship with God.[27] This transcendental or above approach is theocentric in its view towards human being.

1.6.3. Correlation Approach: Paul Tillich offered a 'method of correlation' in which he argues the content of the Christian faith

---

[23] Grenz, *20th Century Theology* ..., p. 50.

[24] Karl Barth, *The Theology of Schleiermacher,* translated by Geoffrey W. Bromiley (Grand Rapids, Michigan: William B. Eerdmans Publishing Company, 1982), p. 187.

[25] Karl Barth, *Church Dogmatics,* vol. III/2 (Edinburgh: T. & T. Clark, 1960), p. 3.

[26] Barth, *Church Dogmatics,* vol. III/2 ..., pp. 72-73.

[27] David Cairns, *The Image of God in Man* (London: SCM Press Ltd., 1953), p. 9.

as the correlation of human existential questions and theological answers. He says that divine-human relationship is a correlation in the sense that God answers human existential questions and under the impact of that answers human being ask questions. The task of theology is to formulate the questions implied in human existence, and to formulate the answers implied in divine self-manifestation under the guidance of the questions implied in human existence. He asserts that "the answers implied in the event of revelation are meaningful only in so far as they are in correlation with questions concerning the whole of our existence, with existential questions."[28] This method of correlation analyzes the human situation with existential questions and demonstrates the symbols used in Christian message as the answers to those questions.[29]

1.6.4. Christological Approach: Proposing a Christological approach, we are critical on both anthropocentric approach and theocentric approach. Moltmann says that Feuerbach's anthropology is an anthropotheism which is divinization of human being. For Feuerbach, the secret of theology is anthropology and this dethroning of God makes human being a God for themselves.[30] He says that divinization makes human being no more human, rather more inhuman.[31] This point of critique could be applied to the theocentric approach as well for it leads to divinization of human being, which is negation of dignity and identity of human being. Traditional understanding of salvation and perfection in terms of divinization is the negation of the dignity and identity of human being. However, in our Christological approach, we are not simply having correlation. James H. Cone argues that truth is not exhausted by the questions we ask. In the encounter with Christ there is the otherness beyond our immediate experience.[32] Therefore, in Christological approach, we

---

[28] Paul Tillich, *Systematic Theology,* vol. I (London: NISBET & Co., Ltd., 1953), p. 69.

[29] Tillich, *Systematic Theology* …, p. 70.

[30] Jurgen Moltmann, *Man: Christian Anthropology in the Conflicts of the Present,* translated by John Sturdy (Minneapolis: Fortress Press, 1974), p. 106.

[31] Moltmann, *Man* …, p. 107.

[32] James H. Cone, *God of the Oppressed* (New York: Orbis Books, 1997), p. 101.

offer to look at Christ, who is the ground of dialectical relationship between distinctive poles, to understand who and what human being is.

1.6.5. Christological Foundation of Theological Anthropology: Jon Sobrino says in line with Blaise Pascal that without Jesus Christ we do not know who God is or who human beings are. He even says that without Jesus Christ we cannot fully know what liberation is or what oppression is. Therefore, Christology needs to immerse itself in the mystery of Christ.[33] John Macquarrie says that understanding of ourselves makes possible of our response to any revelation or recognition of any revelation and the revelation will in turn shed new light on that natural understanding of ourselves. However, one can only understand who human being is when one has seen who Christ is, for it is in the light of Christ and his cross that both the actual sinfulness of man is revealed, and also his potential destiny of sonship. On the other hand, if we do not start from the awareness of our existence, Christ could mean nothing to us.[34] In relation to the thesis of Beyerhaus, M. M. Thomas says that:

I think the ultimate framework of reference for Christian thought is neither God nor man in the abstract, neither the metaphysics of God nor the science of man taken in isolation, but Jesus Christ who is God-Man or rather God-for-Man, or, to use Karl Barth's expression, the Humanity of God. Therefore properly speaking, Christian missionary thinking cannot be either theology or anthropology except as either of them is related to Christology. On the same reasoning, if it is Christ-centered, anthropology could become truly Christian in its framework.[35]

In this regard image of Christ is where we see the true humanity for Christ is the revelation of the mystery of humanity. Therefore, theological anthropology, grounded in Christology, is an understanding of a dialectical relationship between theology and

---

[33] Jon Sobrino, *Jesus the Liberator* (Maryknoll, New York: Orbis Books, 2004), p. 4.

[34] John Macquarrie, *Principles of Christian Theology* (New York: Charles Scribner's Sons, 1966), p. 210.

[35] M. M. Thomas, *Salvation and Humanisation* (Madras: Christian Literature Society, 1971), p. 7.

anthropology. This is also to say that a genuine Christian theological formulation needs to be Christological which must take into account of the relation of theology to the social existence of human being.

1.7. The Mystery of Human Being:

The starting point of theological anthropology is the mystery of human being. It is from where theological anthropology makes its move attempting to find who or what human being is and understands human being as 'human becoming.'

1.7.1. A Quest of Human Being: The question itself, who is human being? is very problematic. Emil Brunner says that when we begin to inquire the nature of ourselves, seeking an answer to our surroundings, it lead us to a more disquieting question. "Not only is the world full of riddles; he himself, who asks the riddles, has become a riddle… This riddle is not the fruit of our opinions; it springs from its own inward necessity."[36] He continues to say that "the human being who knows nothing about his human existence, and does not inquire into it, is not a human being; this existence freed from all questioning is not human but animal existence."[37] For Moltmann, human being asking what is human being? occurs in different contexts. The question 'What is human?,' therefore, always involves a comparison and is never posed in the abstract.[38] He says that questions arise from three comparisons: comparison of human being with animals; with other human being; with the divine.[39] For David H. Kelsey, the question of human being needs to be asked in relation to the non-negotiable claim of Christian faith about how God relates to us. He uses the three questions, "what" "who" and "how" in the light of how God relates to us.[40] This ambiguous nature of human being reflects the mystery of human being and it is from where answers have been sought.

---

[36] Emil Brunner, *Man in Revolt* (Philadelphia: Westminster Press, 1939), p. 17.

[37] Brunner, *Man in Revolt* …, pp. 29-30.

[38] Moltmann, *Man* …, p. 4.

[39] Moltmann, *Man* …, pp. 4-15.

[40] Kelsey, *Eccentric Existence* …, p. 8.

1.7.2. Answer in the Redemption of Christ: Theological anthropology, traditionally, has been constructed on the foundation of the redemption brought by Christ. In the Bible, sin is defined in terms of both religious and moral. In the religious dimension, sin is defined as human being's rebellion against God and the effort to usurp the place of God. On the other hand, the moral and social dimension of sin is defined as injustice.[41] The Pelagian controversy of the early fifth century, which took place between Augustine of Hippo and Pelagius, brought out certain questions on human nature, sin and grace.[42] According to Pelagius, humanity is justified on the basis of merits, which means salvation is the result of good works through human free will. Rejecting the notion of original sin, salvation, for him, is the fulfillment of an obligation laid down by God. Jesus Christ reveals through actions and teaching what God requires of the individual. Salvation in Christ is achieved through imitating the example of Christ.[43]

God decided to give rational creatures the gift of good will and the power of free choice. By making a person naturally capable of good and evil, so that he could do both and would direct his own will to either, God arranged that what an individual actually chose would be properly his own. The good could be done voluntarily only by a creature which was also capable of evil. Therefore the most excellent creator decided to make us capable of both.[44]

However, Augustine, in response to Pelagius, said that God's ineffable gift of heavenly grace enlightens us which opens the eyes of our hearts and shows us the things to come.[45] He says that "Christ's grace has restored us and regenerated us as better persons. His blood has purged and cleansed us; his example spurred us to righteousness.

---

[41] Reinhold Niebuhr, *The Nature and Destiny of Man,* one volume edition (New York: Charles Scribner's Sons, 1949), p. 179.

[42] Alister E. McGrath, *Christian Theology: An Introduction,* third edition (Oxford: Blackwell Publishers Ltd., 2001), p. 443.

[43] McGrath, *Christian Theology* ..., pp. 448-449.

[44] Pelagius, "Letter to Demetrias," in *Theological Anthropology,* translated and edited by J. Patout Burns, (Philadelphia: Fortress Press, 1981), p. 42.

[45] Augustine, "On the Grace of Christ," in *Theological Anthropology* ..., p. 66.

We should be better than people who lived before the law."[46] Here human being is the object matter of our search for humanity and it is the restoration of true humanity through the redemption of Christ.

1.7.3. Answer in Human Self-Understanding: The traditional theological anthropology stands in opposition to L. A. Feuerbach's understanding of humanity as absolute. Heimo Hofmeister says that Feuerbach turned aside from transcendental metaphysics and understood human beings as absolute in itself.[47] Self-understanding and transcendency is one of the essential differences of human being from other creation. Reinhold Niebuhr says that self-consciousness of human being represent human transcendence in which the self is the object whereas the ego is finally always subject. He says that Christianity knows this rational capacity of surveying the world and analyzing the order of the world is one aspect of the "spirit." Thus, the self stands outside itself and the world cannot find meaning of life in the world. "This essential homelessness of the human spirit is the ground of all religion."[48] It is human self-understanding and self-transcendency that makes possibility of the subject matter of human being in the quest of humanity.

1.7.4. Human Being as 'Human Becoming': The question, what is human being? must be addressed in relation to what does it mean to be human being? Gerhard Ebeling says "Only a human being can be inhuman, and even the one who is inhuman has a claim to be treated as human."[49] This shows the right of everyone to claim one's humanity and impossibility to renounce it. However, John Macquarrie suggests that we should not speak of 'human being' but of a 'human becoming'. To say human becoming is possible in the sense that we are discovering, with hope, and realizing the potentials of a human existence. Since, the potentials already belong to us, we, of course, already are human. But the point is "that our humanity is not simply a natural endowment (as

---

[46] Augustine, "On the Grace of Christ," ..., pp. 87-88.

[47] Hofmeister, "Philosophical Anthropology," ..., p. 76.

[48] Niebuhr, *The Nature and Destiny* ..., p. 14.

[49] Gerhard Ebeling, *Dogmatik des christlichen Glaubens*, p. 531. Cited by John Macquarrie, *In Search of Humanity* (London: SCM Pres Ltd; 1982), p. 2.

felinity is to a cat) but has to be discovered and realized."[50] Human being as becoming is also spoken by Ted Peters.

> We may have begun as soil alone but we need not stay that way when we inhale the Spirit of God and gain the freedom to transcend ourselves. Thus, a soil inspired by spirit, we recognize that our life is radically contingent on something bigger and external to us, something that invades and enlivens us, something that by nature is gracious.[51]

The mystery of human being can be understood in terms of human becoming. The human potency of becoming is enhanced by the Christ proleptic event and it is in the relationship of human being with Christ that fullness of humanity will be realized.

1.8. Question on Human Dignity in Theological Anthropology:

Another important issue in theological anthropology comes from the question of human position in relation to God and creation. There can be two models regarding human relation to God and creation:

1.8.1. Human Superiority or Hierarchical Model: When Lactantius (240-320 C.E.) says that God created human being as "sacred animal" (*sanctum animal*) it means that human dignity comes from God's work of creation.[52] According to Theophilus of Antioch, in the act of creation, God reveals the dignity of human being when God declared, "Let us make man after our image and likeness" (Gen 1:26), and appointed him to have dominion over all earthly thing.[53] For Augustine, the image of God is seated in the very soul of human being, which certainly "it always is" even after the fall despite "the disfigurement of its dignity."[54] However,

---

[50] Macquarrie, *In Search of Humanity* ..., p. 2.

[51] Ted Peters, *God The World's Future* (Minneapolis: Fortress Press, 2000), p. 149.

[52] Alexander Roberts and James Donaldson, eds., *The Ante-Nicene Fathers,* vol. 7 (Grand Rapids: Eerdmans, 1971), p. 187.

[53] Theophilus of Antioch, *Ad Autolycum,* text and trans. by Robert M. Grant (Oxford: Clarendon, 1970), p. 57.

[54] Augustine. *On Trinity,* 14.4. (Augustine, *The Trinity,* p. 418.). Cited by R. Kendall Soulen and Linda Woodhead, "Introduction: Contextualizing Human Dignity," in *God and Human Dignity,* ..., p. 5.

Tertullian (c. 160-225 C.E.), in *On the Resurrection*, even speaks of "the dignity of the flesh" not only in God's creation but in the final resurrection.[55] Based on the accounts of creation in the Book of Genesis, Alister E. McGrath says that human being, created in the image of God, is the height of God's creation, set over and above the animal kingdom.[56]

1.8.2. Non-Hierarchical Model: Jurgen Moltmann is strongly reacting against the monotheistic and hierarchical understanding of God. He says that so long as God is the absolute subject, the world is the object of creation. In the absolute monotheistic tradition God, the Creator and Lord of the earth is stripped of connection with the world which results in the cognition of human being, God's image, as ruler over the world. This is the foundation of the hierarchical doctrine of sovereignty.[57] Moltmann, however, in his formulation on the Christian doctrine of creation, intends to relate the word 'Christian' in its original sense as 'messianic' which is directed towards the liberation of human being and nature. In this concept of Messiah, Christ has become the redeemer of the community of human beings and nature from negative powers, and forces of death.[58] He says that Sabbath is the "prefiguration of the world to come." It is only in the Sabbath that creation is completed and crowned with glory. Sabbath is the goal of the Creative God in which people celebrate and perceive the world as God's creation.[59] Against Karl Barth, Moltmann says that "In God there is no one-sided relationship of superiority and subordination, command and obedience, master and servant."[60] He developed the idea of the Trinitarian perichoresis as "reciprocal indwelling and mutual interpenetration" and says

God *in* the world and the world *in* God; heaven and earth *in* the kingdom of God, pervaded by his glory; soul and body united *in* the life-giving Spirit to a human whole; woman and man *in* the

---

[55] Tertullian, *Treatise on the Resurrection,* with text, ed. and trans. by Ernest Evans (London: SPCK, 1960), p. 15.

[56] McGrath, *Christian Theology* ..., p. 440.

[57] Jurgen Moltmann, *God in Creation* (London: SCM Press Ltd., 1985), p. 1.

[58] Moltmann, *God in Creation* ..., pp. 4-5.

[59] Moltmann, *God in Creation* ..., p. 6.

[60] Moltmann, *God in Creation* ..., p. 16.

kingdom of unconditional and unconditional love, freed to be true and complete human beings. There is no such thing as solitary life.[61]

In line with this non-hierarchical model, we attempt to formulate a theological anthropology by placing human being as one of the participants in the divine community that would provide an integrative model of God-human-world relationship.

1.9. 'Image of God' as 'Image of Christ':

The nature and dignity of human being is traditionally understood as grounded in the Image of God. James Luther Mays has rightly pointed out that "Image of God" has always been the central theme of theological anthropology. In Christian theology, since patristic period to modern period, the dignity of human nature is always connected to the theme of the image of God.[62] We will, therefore, highlight various understanding of Image of God, viewing how it has been employed for claiming 'human dignity.' However, we will continue with an understanding of Image of God as 'human identity,' where we will propose an understanding of image of God in terms of 'image of Christ.'

1.9.1. Image of God as Human Dignity: Understanding image of God as human dignity is the question of 'what' human being is. Traditionally, Jesus Christ is understood as the true image of God who is the destiny of human being. H. Russel Botman says that "image and likeness of God" has proven influential in the formation of modern conceptions of human dignity. Humankind posses freedom and reason and must be respected because he or she posses a dignity, being created in the image of God. He says that "According to this reasoning, infringement on human rights amount to violation of image and therefore also of one's likeness to God."[63] Let us discuss various understanding of image of God.

---

[61] Moltmann, *God in Creation* ..., p. 17.

[62] Mays, "The Self in the Psalms and the Image of God," ..., p. 35.

[63] H. Russel Botman, "Covenantal Anthropology: Three Discourses of Human Dignity," in *God and Human Dignity,* edited by R. Kendall Soulen and Linda Woodhead (Grand Rapids: William B. Eerdmans Publishing Company, 2006), p. 83.

1.9.1.1. *Image of God as the ground of human being*: During the early patristic period, a distinction was drawn between "image" and "likeness" of God. Irenaeus and Tertullian find the "image" in bodily traits, and "likeness" in the spiritual nature of human being. However, Clement of Alexandria and Origen rejected the idea of any bodily analogy. They held that the word "image" denoted the characteristics of human as human, and the word "likeness," as the qualities which are not essential to human being, but may be cultivated or lost.[64] For Tertullian, humanity retained the image of God after sinning and could be restored to the likeness of God through the renewing activity of the Holy Spirit. Origen also argued that the term "image of God" referred to humanity after the Fall, while the term "likeness of God" referred to human nature after its perfection at the final consummation.[65]

For Karl Barth, God is revealed in the Word of God and Jesus is the revealing word of God. Jesus is the source of our knowledge about the nature of human being as created by God.[66] We see the World Council of Churches' affirmation in the Faith and Order Paper 199 saying "all human beings are created in the image of God and Jesus Christ is the one in whom true humanity is perfectly realized."[67]

1.9.1.2. *Image of God as rationality*: An understanding of image of God as rationality, which has been discussed from the very early period, is much in connection to the modern emphasis on the autonomy of human reason. Augustine interpreted "the image of God" in terms of human reason. The human rational faculty is the distinction of humanity from the animal kingdom. Though human reason has been corrupted by the Fall, it may be renewed by grace in the knowledge of God according to the image of its creator.[68] This rational theory, as Ted Peters says, believed that human intellect reflects the divine reality. Athanasius, John of Damascus, and Vladimir Soloviev define human being as a rational animal and our

---

[64] L. Berkhof, *Systematic Theology* (Grand Rapids, Michigan: William B. Eerdmans Publishing Co., 1941), p. 202.

[65] McGrath, *Christian Theology* ..., p. 441.

[66] Barth, *Church Dogmatics,* vol. III/2 ..., p. 3.

[67] "Christian Perspectives on Theological Anthropology," ..., p. 2.

[68] McGrath, *Christian Theology* ..., p. 441.

rational capacity corresponds to the divine mind.[69] Thomas Aquinas says that in other creatures we find likeness by way of *trace,* but likeness of *image* is found only in intellect or mind which is possessed by the rational creatures, that is human being. Therefore, the rational creature, human being, alone can possess image of God.[70]

1.9.1.3. ***Image of God as morality*****:** Another understanding of image of God is the original uprightness and dignity of human nature. This understanding of morality is close to the Kantian 'practical reason.'[71] John Wesley says that human beings were created in God's "natural image," which means that we are spiritual beings with free will; we were created in God's political image," which means that we share in the governance over nature. What is most important in that we were created in God's "moral image," which means that humans were filled with love, justice, mercy, and truth at the time of creation before the Fall. We were created originally in God's moral image without knowing evil in any degree.[72]

1.9.1.4. ***Image of God as historicity*****:** The Hegelian understanding of 'truth as process'[73] reflects this understanding of image of God as historicity. Gordon Kaufman explains image of God in terms of historicity. He says that God's act of producing the world is historical, and in history God continues to develop the world. Here, in this cosmic historical process, we see human history and the history of salvation are segments, in some way a

---

[69] Peters, *God The World's Future* ..., p. 153.

[70] Thomas Aquinas, *The Summa Theologica,* Part I. QQ. LXXV – CII, translated by Fathers of the English Dominican Province (London: Burns Oates and Washbourne Ltd., 1920), p. 293.

[71] The foundation of Immanuel Kant's argument is that human being is a moral being, not only a being of sense experience. Human relation is not limited to scientific knowledge; rather the world is a realm of moral value. See Grenz, *20th Centur Theology* ..., p. 28.

[72] Wesley, WW. 6:66; see Charles W. Carter, "Anthropology," in Carter, ed., *A Contemporary Wesleyan Theology,* 2 vols....1:205, 224.). Cited by Peters, *God The World's Future*..., pp. 153-154.

[73] "Hegel linked the truth of reality with the process of history, which he viewed as Spirit coming to self-awareness. In fact, this "whole" is not merely one characteristic of reality; for Hegel it is reality." See Grenz, *20th Century Theology* ..., p. 34.

culmination. Human being, as another historical being, has special significance working out his own purposes and creating further history. Human being, intrinsically historical like God, is capable of entering into communion with God, responding to God creatively and freely. Therefore, the doctrine of imago Dei is in fact a theological explanation of human being, though on the finite level, is in certain respects like God.[74]

Most of these understandings of image of God claim human dignity as standing in the ontological likeness to God. This understanding elevates human being to the level of God at the expense of human identity. For this reason we will look at image of God as human identity.

1.9.2. Image of God as Human Identity: Understanding the Image of God as human identity is a matter of an attempt to understand 'who' human being is. Image of God renewed in the person Jesus Christ means that Jesus Christ does not represent God, but represents human being for image of God is what humanity is as we see in Moltmann. Understanding the image of God in terms of representation on earth, Moltmann argues for the distinction of God and human being. Of all other creatures, human beings are only that has been created and destined as image of God upon the earth. He says that "there are no divine men. Human man is neither 'man's God' nor 'man's wolf,' but is conscious of being a creature of a free God among his fellow-creatures." God wills to be present upon earth and the image, human being, is meant to represent Him and to act in His name. The image of God indicates the special position of human being in the world. Human being is a mirror that shows God's work, social roles, loves and fears.[75]

Lactantius, in his *Divine Institution* (c. 304-11), argued that being created in the image of God established the common identity and dignity of all human beings, which lead to political doctrines concerning human rights and responsibilities.[76] Understanding the image of God as human identity is to claim a distinctive and

---

[74] Gordon Kaufman, *Systematic Theology: A Historical Perspective* (New York: Charles Scribner's Sons, 1968), p. 329.

[75] Moltmann, *Man* ..., p. 109.

[76] McGrath, *Christian Theology* ..., p. 441.

particular identity of human being. However, to equate the image of God with human identity is not a total negation of human dignity. To claim our true dignity we need to be aware of our true identity. Only in the light of our true identity that we can rightly see our true dignity.

1.9.3. Image of God as Image of Christ: It is the affirmation of the World Council of Churches that human beings are called to grow into the image of Christ, who is the true and complete image of God. This is in relation to St. Paul's writings of Christians as reflecting God's glory in the face of Jesus, where he writes in terms of transformation ("from one degree of glory to another," 2 Cor. 3:18).[77] Tertullian understands the image of God as the image of Christ, for Christ is the Word, which is also God, who has to become flesh and that image of Christ is fulfilled in Jesus.

For the Father had already spoken to the Son in these words, *Let us make man unto our own image and likeness. And God made man* (the same thing of course as 'formed'): *unto the image of God* ('of Christ', it means) *made he him.* For the Word also is God, who being in the form of God thought it not robbery to be equal with God. (Cf. Phil 2:6) Thus, that clay, already putting on the image of Christ who was to be in the flesh, was not only a work of God but also a token of him.[78]

As James Luther Mays uses the title "Jesus as call and Promise of Representation and Likeness," he explains that Jesus is understood as the one who precedes the existence of all that was created and was the destiny of human being as image of God. "Christ Jesus so absolutely preempts the role of image of God that the vocation and destiny of human beings can be realized only through a transformation of their existence by his spirit (2 Cor. 3:1-8)."[79] Here we see that Christ is the representation of image of God that is the true identity of human being. However, image of God manifests in Jesus Christ does not mean that Jesus Christ is image of God. Jesus Christ represents the true and full image of God.

---

[77] "Christian Perspectives on Theological Anthropology" ..., pp. 14-15.

[78] Tertullian, *Treatise on the Resurrection* ..., p. 19.

[79] Mays, "The Self in the Psalms and the Image of God," ..., p. 41.

Jon Sobrino, in his book *Jesus the Liberator,* presents the image of Christ through the life of Jesus of Nazareth and called "Jesus the liberator." He says that a new image of Christ (liberator) could be retrieved by returning to Jesus of Nazareth.[80] Here is the point that image of God, which is human being (not Christ), is realized through image of Christ.

1.10. Conclusion:

As Christian theology envisions the image of Christ as the horizon of human becoming, Christian anthropology needs to be grounded in Christology. We, therefore, need to engage with the Christological frameworks for our discussion on theological anthropology. The main hypothesis is to formulate a theological anthropology having our foundation on the image of Christ. This is our hermeneutical shift of looking at human being as the image of God in order to bring out a systematic and meaningful theological formulation for our time. We attempt to understand the image of God in terms of representation, which is seeking an identity without claiming human dignity that looks at ontological image of God. Drawing our attention to how Christ represents and reveals the true identity of human being, we will explore the person and work of Christ in Friedrich Schleiermacher and Raimond Panikkar in chapter two and chapter three, respectively.

---

[80] Sobrino, *Jesus the Liberator* ..., p. 1.

Chapter 2

'Perfection and Blessedness' in the Christology of Friedrich Schleiermacher

2.1. Introduction:

In the first chapter, we have argued that Christian anthropology needs to be grounded in Christology and suggest the image of Christ as the hermeneutical device for understanding human being. It is, now, our task to explore the humanity revealed in Christ. In this chapter, we will be looking at Friedrich Schleiermacher, who is mostly hailed as the 'Father of modern theology.'[81]

We will be looking at the context and background in which Schleiermacher developed his thought. A brief discussion on his life and experience, which were truly embedded in his theological formulation, will be made. We will also be dealing with his two major works that truly reflect his thought on the true essence of religion and basic Christian teachings. Since, his understanding of religion, the essence, is constitutive of his whole theological reflection, we will also be looking at his various thoughts to help us in understanding him better.

[81] Grenz, *20th Century Theology* ..., p. 39.

However, our central focus will be on Schleiermacher's understanding of Christ with an intention to see how the nature of humanity is reflected in the person and work of Christ. We will, then, reflect on the Christological foundation of humanity through his understanding of Christ.

2.2. The Context and Background:

There were various historical events that occurred during the lifetime of Friedrich Daniel Ernst Schleiermacher. Stephen Sykes mentioned some of those events and said that it was just before the American war of independence (1776-1783) that Schleiermacher was born. The influence of the industrial revolution of the eighteenth century could be felt throughout his life. When Schleiermacher was 10, the French revolution broke out and when he was 38, a university professor, Prussia was overrun by Napoleon. The influence of all these events in the life of Schleiermacher was not doubtful.[82] Apart from these events there were two significant intellectual factors that had influence and contributed to the thought of Friedrich Schleiermacher:

2.2.1. The Enlightenment: The *Encyclopedia of Christian Theology* says that the term "Enlightenment" signifies the dominant rationalist and liberal cultural movement that occurred in Europe from roughly 1690 to the French Revolution (1789). The term could be traced back to Bernard Le Bovier de Fontenelle's (1657-1757) *History of the Renewal of the Royal Academy of Sciences* where he referred to the major development in all the arts, and above all in philosophy. Certain characteristics of the Enlightenment were the empirical investigation in the sciences, its optimism about progress in all realms of life, and its belief in human perfectibility.[83]

In *The Cambridge Dictionary of Christian Theology,* we see that the term "enlightenment" is an intellectual catchword for a historical epoch, broadly eighteenth century Europe, as well as a set of philosophical tenets and moral sensibilities articulated within this era. With antecedents, J. Locke's (1632–1704) advocacy of natural

[82] Stephen Sykes, *Friedrich Schleiermacher* (Atlanta: John Knox Press, 1971), p. 1.

[83] Anthony Levi, "Enlightenment," in *Encyclopedia of Christian Theology,* edited by Jean Yves Lacoste, vol. 1 (A – F) (New York, London: Routledge, 2005), p. 477.

religion, and R. Descartes' (1596–1650) quest for a principle of human certitude, Enlightenment thought flourished in England, Scotland, Germany, and among the philosophers in pre-revolutionary France.[84]

Immanuel Kant explained that "Enlightenment is man's leaving his self-caused immaturity. Immaturity is the incapacity to use one's intelligence without the guidance of another... Have the courage to use your own intelligence! is therefore the motto of the enlightenment."[85] He said that what is required for enlightenment is the *freedom* for human being to make public use of reason in all matters and at all times.[86] The main point of enlightenment is the release of human being from self-caused immaturity primarily in matters of religion.[87] The closing years of the eighteenth century has been pointed as the end of the Enlightenment Era. By the time Immanuel Kant published his *Critique of Pure Reason* (1791) the Age of Reason had run its course.[88]

2.2.2. Romanticism: *The Encyclopedia of Christianity* explains that 'Romanticism' is an intellectual and artistic movement associated with the fervor of revolutionary change in all Europe and the United States during the latter third of the 18th and the first third of the 19th century. It is characterized by certain shifts: from matter based physics to energy physics; materialism to idealism; mimetic to subjective expression; monarchical authority to democratic; ecclesiastical dogma to intuitive. Romanticism, though, pervasive it did not swept away all opposition and instigated polemical conflict and ideological faction.[89] Shaped by the rationalist impasse of the

---

[84] Richard Crouter, "Enlightenment," in *The Cambridge Dictionary of Christian Theology*, edited by Ian A. McFarland, et al. (New York: Cambridge University Press, 2011), p. 164.

[85] Carl J. Friedrich, ed., *The Philosophy of Kant* (New York: The Modern Library, 1949), p. 132.

[86] Friedrich, *The Philosophy of Kant* ..., p. 134.

[87] Friedrich, *The Philosophy of Kant* ..., p. 138.

[88] Grenz, *20th Century Theology* ..., p. 17.

[89] Frederick Burwick, "Romanticism," in *The Encyclopedia of Christianity*, edited by Erwin Fahlbusch, et al., vol. 4 (Grand Rapids, Michigan: Willian B. Eerdmans Publishing Company, 2005), pp. 741-742.

Enlightenment, the Romantics argued that religion could not be grounded on reason alone. Some became skeptical to the extent that they dismissed the church as corrupt and religion as hoax. However, some other argued for the accessibility to divinity through feeling or intuition, immanent in nature or within the self.[90]

According to Richard B. Brandt, the German romanticist's attitude towards life is that Human being is not fallen but is the crown of the universe and not opposed to the world, the highest production of spirit and mind is the essence. Right conduct was viewed as the free expression of the spiritual nature of human being. He says that the root of romanticism, as Kircher writes, is the idealism of humanity and the power of soul is the eternal goodness of the inward being which is faith in the inward God.[91] In Schlegel's writings we have "the infinity of the human soul," "the divinity of all natural things, and the humanity of gods, remain the great eternal themes of all these variations."[92]

Brandt says that the romanticist's attitude towards the world depends upon the 'transcendental idealist.' He says, Walzel has pointed out that the romanticist were not purely artists for philosophical problems are always in the background of their ideas and romanticism is "unthinkable without Kant, although the antithesis to Kant gives the movement its proper claim to existence."[93] The Romantic tenets like, reconciliation of human being with nature and God, reason with sensuous, and confidence in the divinity of human nature seem to be the direct antithesis to the moralism of Kant and Fichte.[94]

---

[90] Burwick, "Romanticism," in *The Encyclopedia of Christianity* ..., p. 752.

[91] Richard B. Brandt, *The Philosophy of Schleiermacher* (New York and London: Harper & Brothers Publishers, 1941), p. 61.

[92] Karl Wilhelm Friedrich Schlegel was a critical leader of German Romanticism born in 1772 – 1829. See *Athenaeum,* vol. I, p. 35. Cited in Brandt, *The Philosophy of Schleiermacher* ..., pp. 61-62.

[93] O. F. Walzel, *Deutsche Romantick*, vol. I. p. 25. Cited by Brandt, *The Philosophy of Schleiermacher* ..., p. 62.

[94] Brandt, *The Philosophy of Schleiermacher* ..., p. 62.

2.3. Schleiermacher's Life and Experience:

2.3.1. Early Life: Schleiermacher was born in Breslau, Lower Silesia. He grew up among the pietistic traditions of the Moravian Brethren (Herrnhuter) of southern Saxony, founded by Count Nicholas L. von Zinzendorf in 1722.[95] He was born on November 21, 1768, by that time his father Gottlied Schleiermacher was a Reformed chaplain in Silesia.[96]

2.3.2. Early Education and Skepticism: His parents resolved that their children's education should be entrusted to the schools of the Moravian Brethren. Schleiermacher entered the Moravian school in Niesky on June 14, 1783, and then he became a Moravian outwardly and inwardly. During this time of his studies, the Moravian Brethren devotion to Jesus became very important in his life. The Brethren not only wanted the students to learn about the Christian teaching of sin and grace, but to experience the presence of God within the most inner recesses of the self.[97] On September 17, 1785, he left Niesky for Barby and arrived on September 22, 1785, after five days of journey by foot.[98] At Barby seminary, he studied Greek, Latin, Hebrew, French, English and mathematics including the experiential, biblical and Jesus-centered piety of the Brethren. In that seminary he took part in a club where Emmanuel Kant and Goethe were read and debated. He became skeptical about whether Jesus was the Son of Man was the true, eternal God and whether Jesus' death was a vicarious atonement because Jesus himself never said so. Schleiermacher, in his letter to his father, said that God did not create human being for perfection, but for the pursuit of it, and cannot punish them eternally just because they have not attained it. His inability to obtain clear answer to these religious doubts led him

---

[95] Richard Crouter, "Introduction: *On Religion* in Its Cultural Mileu," in Friedrich Schleiermacher, *On Religion: Speeches to its Cultured Despisers,* trans. and ed. by Richard Crouter, Cambridge Text in the History of Philosophy (London: Cambridge University Press, 1996), p. xii.

[96] Martin Redeker, *Schleiermacher: Life and Thought,* translated by John Wallhausser (Philadelphia: Fortress Press, 1973), p. 7.

[97] Redeker, *Schleiermacher: Life and Thought* ..., pp. 9-10.

[98] Redeker, *Schleiermacher: Life and Thought* ..., p. 12.

to a painful exchange of letters with his father and was transferred to the University of Halle.[99]

2.3.3. Conversion and Spiritual Reformation: When Schleiermacher, being born into a devout family, was nine years old, his father, an army chaplain, underwent a spiritual awakening. Five years later, Schleiermacher, too, experienced a conversion while he was at school among the Moravians.[100] After his mother's death, he moved to the Moravian seminary and there reached the crisis point of his spiritual troubles. When his father said that faith is the "regalia of the Godhead," Schleiermacher confessed that:

Faith is the regalia of the Godhead, you say. Alas! Dearest father, if you believe that without this faith no one can attain to salvation in the next world, nor to tranquility in this – and such, I know is our belief –oh! then pray to God to grant it to me, for to me it is now lost. I cannot believe that he who called himself the Son of Man was the true, eternal God; I cannot believe that his death was vicarious atonement.[101]

Terrible was the father's reaction saying that his son (Schleiermacher) has crucified Christ, it disturbed his late mother's rest, and made his step-mother weep. He was straying to earn honors of the world. And his father said "I must, for you no longer worship the God of your father, no longer kneel at the same alter with him."[102] However, Gerrish commented that Schleiermacher did not lose faith in Christ but his first understanding of it. This is clearly proved by *The Christian Faith,* where he criticized orthodox doctrines, everything still hangs on the picture of the Savior and its compelling attraction. After he dropped out of seminary and attended rationalist University of Halle, reconciliation with his father eventually took place.[103]

Schleiermacher took his first ordination exam in 1790. On 16th August 1791, he wrote a cheering news to his father that "My heart

---

[99] Schleiermacher, *On Religion* ..., p. xii.

[100] B. A. Gerrish, *A Prince of the Church: Schleiermacher and the Beginnings of Modern Theology* (Philadelphia: Fortress Press, 1984), p. 24.

[101] Schleiermacher's letter to his father sent on 21st January, 1787. Cited by Gerrish, *A Prince of the Church* ..., p. 25.

[102] Gerrish, *A Prince of the Church* ..., p. 25.

[103] Gerrish, *A Prince of the Church* ..., p. 26.

is properly cultivated ... and is not left to wither under the burden of cold erudition, and my religious feelings are not deadened by theological inquiries."[104] There is a contrast between the religious feelings of the heart and the reflection of the intellect, but they can very well live together. In 1802, after the death of his father, he paid a return visit to the community of the Moravian Brethren and wrote:[105]

Here it was that for the first time I awoke to the consciousness of the relations of man to a higher world... Here it was that that mystic tendency developed itself, which has been of so much importance to me, and has supported and carried me through all the storms of skepticism... And I may say, that after all that I have passes through, I have become a Herrnhuter (Moravian) again, only of a higher order.[106]

2.4. The Two Major Works:

The two major works of Schleiermacher clearly reflect his theological position and nature of his work:

2.4.1. On Religion: Speeches to Its Cultured Despisers (1799): C.W. Christian says that the nineteenth century was confronted with the question whether theology was any longer possible or whether Christian theology was possible. In such a situation, Schleiermacher's work could have been understood as a response to these questions. Christian says that if faith and theology was to be rehabilitated, it would require: finding new authority for faith; demonstrating how the work of theology is to be done; and showing what a theology, which is modern and genuinely Christian, has to say.[107] Schleiermacher had a threefold theological quest which is reflected in *On Religion: Speeches to Its Cultured Despisers*. They are "(1) a search for authority, (2) a reconstruction of theological method, and (3) a reformulation of the

[104] Schleiermacher's letter to his father sent on 16th August, 1791. Cited by Gerrish, *A Prince of the Church* ..., p. 26.

[105] Gerrish, *A Prince of the Church* ..., p. 26.

[106] Schleiermacher's letter to his father sent in 1802 after visiting the community of the Moravian Brethren. Cited by Gerrish, *A Prince of the Church* ..., p. 26.

[107] C. W. Christian, *Friedrich Schleiermacher: Makers of the Modern Theological Mind* (Texas: Word Books Publisher, 1979), p. 43.

content of religious faith in general and of the Christian faith in particular."[108] Generally *Speeches* is regarded as addressing not to the hostile critics of religion but to those, whom he called as "cultured despisers," who concluded human community and value could be achieved without reference to traditional religion and to God. These people were whom he knew in Berlin, who remained sensitive to the deeper dimensions of life to which faith always had pointed.[109]

Richard Crouter says that this book (*On Religion*) reflects the tensions between the religious thought of the Enlightenment and Romanticism. Religion is understood as rooted in pre-reflexive feeling and intuition which arose from the Romantics' critique of Kant's moral and religious philosophy. It was the time of repressive political atmosphere of a Prussia that feared the social upheavals of the French revolution.[110] Rudolf Otto, who wrote the introduction of the book, says

The intention of the work was crystal clear. It aimed to recapture the position religion had lost in the intellectual world where it was now threatened with total oblivion. It aimed to lead religion out of the remote corner into which it had been cast, to prove that religion was not just a concern of the "uncultured" and of old-fashioned people who found in it an emergency substitute for the higher things of life, but something that belonged to truly cultured, authentic, and well-rounded human beings; moreover, that without religion the intellectual life of mankind would deprive itself of its noblest ingredient. The book had been written for the purpose of restoring religion as a ferment and as a prime factor in the growth and further development of the modern age.[111]

2.4.2. The Christian Faith (1821/22): C. W. Christian says that between the publication of the *Speeches* (1799) and the first edition of *The Christian Faith* (1822-23) it could be seen that Schleiermacher was moving into the life of the university. Schleiermacher's deeper

---

[108] Christian, *Friedrich Schleiermacher* ..., p. 44.

[109] Christian, *Friedrich Schleiermacher* ..., p. 45.

[110] Schleiermacher, *On Religion* ..., p. xi.

[111] Rudolf Otto, "Introduction," in Friedrich Schleiermacher, *On Religion: Speeches to its Cultured Despisers,* translated by John Oman (New York: Harper & Brothers, 1958), p. ix.

involvement with the life of the church, his religious and scientific interest are conjoined in the highest degree which resulted in the publication of *The Christian Faith.*[112] He began his lectures on hermeneutics in the summer semester of 1805. With his practical experience in the translation of Plato, he further developed critical interpretation and entered upon the teaching of dogmatic theology. He published *Kurze Darstellung des theologischen Studiums* (*Brief Outline of the Study of Theology*) in 1811.[113] After the seizure of the city of Halle and the dissolution of the university by order of the French conqueror, we see the deeper involvement with the life of the church as he crystallized his ideas on the nature of Protestantism.[114] He left Halle to settle in Berlin, where he became a preacher and participated in the founding of the university. He emerged as defender of the rights of the church against the state as he deepened and increased the scope of his critical and systematic power through is lectures in the university on hermeneutics, ethics, philosophy and theology. Then, *The Christian Faith,* which is much more systematic than those previous works, was published in 1821/22, revised form in 1830/31.[115] Martin Redeker says that *The Christian Faith* is different from the customary organization of dogmatic systems. It has a monistic tendency because of its view of God as the cause of everything. However, the main part of *The Christian Faith* is dualistic antithesis of sin and grace. It is arranged around the human need for redemption and the actual redemption by Christ.[116]

2.5. His Thought:

A precise understanding of Schleiermacher's thought require our attention on his two important approaches: Historicity and Dialectical.

[112] Christian, *Friedrich Schleiermacher* ..., p. 76.

[113] Richard R. Niebuhr, *Schleiermacher on Christ and Religion* (London: SCM Press Ltd, 1964), p. 24.

[114] Niebuhr, *Schleiermacher on Christ* ..., pp. 25-26.

[115] Niebuhr, *Schleiermacher on Christ* ..., p. 27.

[116] Redeker, *Schleiermacher: Life and Thought* ..., p. 109.

2.5.1. Historicity: Schleiermacher distinguishes between three kinds of historiography:

2.5.1.1. *Atomic approach*: The 'atomistic approach' produces at best chronological record, but it fails to demonstrate a connection between historical events or actions. For Schleiermacher, it is a vain curiosity and he rejects this approach.[117]

2.5.1.2. *Pragmatic or Psychological approach*: The 'pragmatic or psychological approach' attempts to explain present events by linking them to causes in the past. Here, Schleiermacher is critical that no one can separate the present from the past as if they were opposites and no one can detach certain parts from the present. It is not caused by a similar single corresponding factor but by a part of all single factors of the recent past.[118]

2.5.1.3. *Organic approach*: For him, the true understanding of history is an 'organic approach' which is to believe that "in history all is one." It is not possible to separate any part from the whole. History is everything that is bound to time, such as natural history, moral history and world history. For Schleiermacher history is all that goes on in the world as a process of becoming and the historian's involvement in this process.[119]

Schleiermacher described history in the *Brief Outline* clearly that "Every historical mass may be viewed (a) on the one hand as one indivisible being and doing in process of becoming, and (b) on the other hand, as a compound of innumerable individual moments. Genuinely historical observation consists in the combination of both"[120] For Schliermacher, Pauck says, history has a goal and it is not an accidental. He speaks of the finite as being on the way (*im unterwegssein*) towards the infinite. The goal of history is "the triumph of life over death," through the "redeeming work of eternal love." In *The Christian Faith,* Schleiermacher interprets Christianity

[117] Wilhelm Pauck, "Schleiermacher's Conception of History and Church History," in *Schleiermacher as Contemporary,* edited by Robert W. Funk (New York: Herder and Herder, 1970), p. 43.

[118] Pauck, "Schleiermacher's Conception of History ..., p. 44.

[119] Pauck, "Schleiermacher's Conception of History ..., p. 44.

[120] Friedrich Schleiermacher, *Brief Outline on the Study of Theology,* sec. 150 (Richmond: John Knox Press, 1966), p. 60.

as a teleological religion. The redemption of all human being is viewed as a gradual progress that it will be accomplished through the communication of Christ's perfect God-consciousness to them.[121] Schleiermacher says that "redemption is being ever more completely realized in time, and the Holy Spirit is thus pervading the whole ever more perfectly..."[122]

2.5.2. Dialectical: Gerhard Spiegler says that, between 1811 -1831, Schleiermacher delivered his lectures on dialectics six times at the University of Berlin. It is in the *Dialectic* that Schleiermacher tries to work out the harmony between his "most intimate religious sensations" and his "deepest speculative thoughts." He also tries to discover the term "eternal covenant" between the Christian faith and culture. He shows himself as a citizen of two worlds, old and new, past and future. The central concern of his dialectical speculation is that all speculative questions can be reduced to the "question of the relationship between God and the world."[123]

2.5.2.1. *Co-inhering polarity/togetherness of opposites*: In the world we observe the phenomenon of unity in diversity and continuity in discontinuity which Schleiermacher accepts as irreducible empirical phenomenon of "co-inhering polarity."[124] Schleiermacher observes the interconnectedness of antitheses that there is polar duality in knowledge as well as in being which cannot be resolved into "simply identity" and "sheer difference." He asserts "togetherness of opposites" is a fundamentally given phenomenon. The co-inhering polarities like universality and particularity, community and individuality, ideality and reality, the intellectual and the organic, spirit and body are present in the world and knowledge requires polar duality. In pursuit of an absolute, the transcendental

---

[121] Pauck, "Schleiermacher's Conception of History ..., p. 46.

[122] Friedrich Schleiermacher, *The Christian Faith*, edited by H. R. Mackintosh and J. S. Stewart (Edinburgh: T & T Clark, 1928), p. 595.

[123] Gerhard Spiegler, "Theological Tensions in Schleiermacher's *Dialectic*," in *Schleiermacher as Contemporary*, edited by Robert W. Funk (New York: Herder and Herder, 1970), p. 15.

[124] Spiegler, "Theological Tensions ..., p. 16.

presupposition of coinhering polarity is attained. Nothing can be predicated except that it is the presupposition of knowledge.[125]

2.5.2.2. *Dialectic existence*: In the first two speeches in *On Religion*, "Defense" and "The Nature of Religion," Schleiermacher is seeking to discover a dimension of experience which is the universal ground of piety, the source and object of all religious devotion. Though universal, it is varied in particular expression.[126] Two moments coexist in everything; a moment of individuation and a moment of participation in the whole of being. This dialectic of individuation and participation manifests in human experience as the awareness of self and world. This relation of self and world is twofold, such as passive and active. In the passive aspect, the world flows into the self, shaping it and giving it substance. In the active aspect, the self acts upon and determines the world. We are not merely objective observers, but subjective shapers, not merely rational beings but volitional beings.[127]

2.6. Understanding of Religion:

Schleiermacher's understanding of religion is one of the important contributions in the field of religious thought and is an outstanding theological undertaking.

2.6.1. True Essence of Religion: Schleiermacher says that religion is essentially contemplative, but this contemplation is not turned to the existence of a finite thing. It is the contemplation of the pious that is "the immediate consciousness of the universal existence of all finite things, in and through the Infinite, and to all temporal things in and through the Eternal."[128] Religion is to seek and find the Infinite "in all that lives and moves, in all growth and change, in all doing and suffering. It is to have life and to know life in immediate feeling, only as such an existence in the Infinite and Eternal."[129] He explains that religion is neither knowledge nor

[125] Spiegler, "Theological Tensions ..., p. 17.

[126] Christian, *Friedrich Schleiermacher* ..., pp. 49-50.

[127] Christian, *Friedrich Schleiermacher* ..., p. 50.

[128] Schleiermacher, *On Religion* ..., p. 36.

[129] Schleiermacher, *On Religion* ..., p. 36.

science, neither world nor God, it recognizes knowledge and science. "In itself it is an affection, a revelation of the Infinite in the finite, God being seen in it and it in God."[130]

However, C. W. Christian says that Schleiermacher's choice of feeling as most akin to religion reflects his years among the Moravians. He still valued the piety and also shared the romantics' dissatisfaction with rationalism. What Schleiermacher is trying to point in feeling is beyond the particular ebb and flow, but "to the deeper ground of all feelings in the awareness of personal continuity and unity – that is, to the abiding consciousness of selfhood."[131]

In *The Christian Faith,* we have a clearer concept and deeper grasp of the implication of his view. He explains the piety as "neither a Knowing nor a Doing, but a modification of Feeling, or of immediate self consciousness."[132] He explains life as the antithesis between an abiding-in-self (*Insichbleiben*) and a passing-beyond-self (*Aussichheraustreten*). The two forms of consciousness, Knowing and Feeling constitute the abiding-in-self, while Doing is the passing-beyond-self which means that Knowing and Feeling stand together in antithesis to Doing. But in the sense of possessing knowledge, Knowing is on the part of the subject and becomes real by a passing-beyond-self of the subject, which is a Doing. In this sense Feeling stands alone in antithesis to the other two – Knowing and Doing.[133]

Feeling is the one to which piety belongs… that piety is excluded from all connexion with Knowing and Doing. For, indeed, it is the case in general that the immediate self-consciousness is always the mediating link in the transition between moments in which Knowing predominates and those in which Doing predominates, so that a different Doing may proceed from the same Knowing in different people according as a different determination of self-consciousness enters in.[134]

2.6.2. The Peculiar Essence of Christianity: Since all other religions share the feeling of absolute dependence, there is a danger to

---

130 Schleiermacher, *On Religion …*, p. 36.

131 Christian, *Friedrich Schleiermacher …*, p. 55.

132 Schleiermacher, *The Christian Faith*, sec. 3 …, p. 5.

133 Schleiermacher, *The Christian Faith …*, p. 8.

134 Schleiermacher, *The Christian Faith …*, pp. 8-9.

subsume Christianity under the general category of religion. However, Schleiermacher is seeking the peculiar essence of Christianity among other religions.

2.6.2.1. *Redemption accomplished by Jesus of Nazareth*: The main peculiar essence of Christianity, Schleiermacher says, is "Christianity is a monotheistic faith, belonging to the teleological type of religion, and is essentially distinguished from other such faiths by the fact that in it everything is related to the redemption accomplished by Jesus of Nazareth."[135] Here, Schleiermacher uses the term redemption, with presupposition that it is the term what all others also confess, as which has been universally and completely accomplished by Jesus of Nazareth. Christian piety could not be said by any means attributable to everyone who is conscious of being in the process of redemption. However, redemption is referred as in Christian consciousness for the redeemer, Jesus, who is the originator of the Christian communion. Every member of the religious communion, founded by Jesus, becomes conscious of redemption through Him.[136]

2.6.2.2. *Antithesis of Sin and Grace: Sin and Redemption*: Walter E. Wyman, Jr. says that 'Sin and redemption' constitute the heart of Schleiermacher's understanding of Christianity.[137] The essential distinction of Christianity from others is the redemption accomplished by Jesus of Nazareth unto which everything is related.[138] The distinctive feature of Christian piety is the antithesis of the consciousness of sin and grace. We are conscious of "alienation from God" that is "an action originating in ourselves, which we call Sin;" at the same time, we are conscious of "fellowship with God" that rests upon a "communication from the Redeemer, which we call Grace."[139]

---

[135] Schleiermacher, *The Christian Faith*, sec. 11 ..., p. 52.

[136] Schleiermacher, *The Christian Faith* ..., p. 56.

[137] Walter E. Wyman, Jr., "Sin and Redemption," in *The Cambridge Companion to Friedrich Schleiermacher*, edited by Jacqueline Marina (New York: Cambridge University Press, 2005), p. 129.

[138] Schleiermacher, *The Christian Faith*, sec. 11 ..., p. 52.

[139] Schleiermacher, *The Christian Faith*, sec. 63 ..., p. 262.

2.7. Understanding of Christ:

Schleiermacher says that "the peculiar activity and the exclusive dignity of the Redeemer imply each other, and are inseparably one in the self-consciousness of believers."[140] This is to say that the division of doctrines into two: the person of Christ and the work of Christ, though are different, but their content is the same.[141]

2.7.1. The Person of Christ: When Schleiermacher speaks of Christ as "an historical individual he must have been at the same time ideal and each historical moment of his experience must at the same time have borne within it the ideal,"[142] he is to say the exemplary dignity and ideality of Christ. He says that the redeemer is like all other human being in his human identity, but distinguished from all others by the constant potency of His God-consciousness, which is the very indwelling presence of God in Jesus.[143] This special presence of the creative power of God in Jesus is His ideality (*Urbildlichkeit*).

Schleiermacher is critical about the classical doctrine of Jesus' two natures (human and divine). He says that it is not possible to have unity of life coexist with the duality of natures.[144] In place of the two natures, he speaks of the concept of Jesus' *Urbildlichkeit* and *Vorbildlichkeit,* the ideality and exemplary dignity. These two aspects of Jesus cannot be separated. By virtue of His ideality, He is the Redeemer and by virtue of His exemplary status, He communicates Redemption. The exemplary status of Jesus (*Vorbildlichkeit*) does not signify life-giving power but signify His solidarity with the human race, apart from which there could be no communication of redemption.[145] However, this solidarity or activity that belongs to the general aspect of human nature is not to reduce the activity to the same measure as that of others. Faith in Christ postulates Christ's

[140] Schleiermacher, *The Christian Faith*, sec. 92 …, p. 374.

[141] Schleiermacher, *The Christian Faith* …, p. 376.

[142] Schleiermacher, *The Christian Faith*, sec. 93 …, p. 377.

[143] Schleiermacher, *The Christian Faith*, sec. 94 …, p. 385.

[144] Schleiermacher, *The Christian Faith* …, p. 393.

[145] Niebuhr, *Schleiermacher on Christ* …, p. 226.

relation to the whole human race and this relation to the whole human race is sufficient to prove the peculiar activity of Christ.[146]

Schleiermacher argues that "In Jesus Christ divine nature and human nature were combined into one person."[147] He says that there is confusion with the expression 'Jesus Christ.' It was used to indicate the eternal divine nature of the Redeemer, before its union with the human nature, so that this union no longer appears as an element that goes to constitute the person, Jesus Christ, but rather as an act of this person Himself. Through this misuse of the expression 'Jesus Christ,' it became a single proper name. But Christ is only the description of the real dignity added to the proper name.[148]

2.7.2. The Works of Christ: The works of Christ is understood as His assumption into the fellowship with Him in terms of both Redemption and reconciliation.

2.7.2.1. *Redemption*: Schleiermacher says that "The Redeemer assumes believers into the power of His God consciousness, and this is His redemptive activity."[149] According to Schleiermacher, the Christian self-consciousness is the act of the Redeemer because His peculiar work first evokes us. This means that Redeemer's activity precedes activity of our own and assumes us into the fellowship of His activity and His life. Schleiermacher says that His act in us can never be anything but the act of His sinlessness and perfection as conditioned by the being of God in Him which becomes ours as we have fellowship of the Redeemer. In the fellowship with the Redeemer, the impulses flow to us from Him and this is where we find in Him from which everything proceeds to be the source of our activity.[150] The redeeming activity of Christ which exhibits it as the establishment of a new life common to Him and us is usually called 'mystical' by those who have not had the experience.[151]

2.7.2.2. *Reconciliation*: Schleiermacher says that "the Redeemer assumes the believers into the fellowship of His

---

[146] Schleiermacher, *The Christian Faith* ..., p. 386.

[147] Schleiermacher, *The Christian Faith,* sec. 96 ..., p. 391.

[148] Schleiermacher, *The Christian Faith* ..., pp. 391-392.

[149] Schleiermacher, *The Christian Faith,* sec. 100 ..., p. 425.

[150] Schleiermacher, *The Christian Faith* ..., p. 425.

[151] Schleiermacher, *The Christian Faith* ..., pp. 428-429.

unclouded blessedness, and this is His reconciling activity."[152] Just as the corporate activity corresponding to the being of God in Him is brought about for all believers by the redemptive activity of Christ, a corporate feeling of blessedness is brought about for all believers by the blessedness of the being of God in Him, which is the reconciling element.[153]

2.8. Christological Foundation of Humanity:

As for Schleiermacher "the appearance of Christ and the institution of this new corporate life" is regarded as the completion of the creation of human nature.[154] Second Adam is like all those who are descended from the first, but has an absolutely potent God-consciousness. He enters the historical order of human nature to bring to perfection the consciousness of sinfulness and to remove the misery. So, He stands under the law of historical development, and that activity is brought to perfection through gradual expansion, from the point at which He appears, over the whole.[155] With this understanding of Christ as the completion of human nature let us see how Richard Niebuhr summarizes Schleiermacher:

2.8.1. Christ as the Ideal and Measure of Human Nature: Richard Niebuhr says that Schleiermacher, in *The Christian Faith,* regards the datum of humanity under the aspect of the form of Christ.[156] The problem of religion is also the problem of human nature. As the matter of religion is human nature, the relation of Christianity to religion is also the relation of Christ to human nature.[157] He, therefore, named Schleiermacher's theology as 'Christo-morphic' in two senses: Firstly, Jesus of Nazareth is the ideal human nature and is the measure of human nature. Secondly, Jesus is the historical person whose presence mediated through Scriptures and preaching. Holy Spirit abides in the reorganization of Christian's consciousness of his

[152] Schleiermacher, *The Christian Faith*, sec. 101 ..., p. 431.

[153] Schleiermacher, *The Christian Faith* ..., p. 433.

[154] Schleiermacher, *The Christian Faith,* sec. 89 ..., pp. 365-366.

[155] Schleiermacher, *The Christian Faith* ..., p. 367.

[156] Niebuhr, *Schleiermacher on Christ* ..., p. 210.

[157] Niebuhr, *Schleiermacher on Christ* ..., p. 211.

absolute dependence. The Redeemer is presented in *The Christian Faith* as the one in whom "Adam" is finally formed.[158]

2.8.2. Christ's Person Forming Activity: Schleiermacher asserts Jesus Christ as the second Adam and the redeeming work of Christ is a "person-forming" work. Christ creates person in the sense that through the communication of His own life in deed and word He brings them into complete existence as human beings and as having particular identities.[159] The being of God in Christ was developed out of human nature and the possibility of drawing down the divine to human nature is innate in it. Therefore, the human nature can have been assumed by the divine only as engaged in a person-forming activity. In the implanting of the divine in the human nature, the human nature was only receptive and could only take a passive part. But as Christ none the less was also perfectly human person, the formation of this person also must have been an act of the human nature; and so the whole process must have been a common act of the two natures.[160] Schleiermacher says that "Christ even as a human person was ever coming to be simultaneously with the world itself."[161] Niebuhr, therefore, says that the forming of human nature into its ordained inner proportions and the regeneration of human being is a being conformed to the image of Christ. The term *Christo-morphism* is to describe the thrust of Schleiermacher's theological thinking about the redeemer, redemption and the redeemed.[162]

2.9. Humanity in the Light of Christ's Perfection and Blessedness:

Looking at Schleiermacher's understanding of Christ, let us draw some insights to understand what it means to be human being.

2.9.1. The primacy of Essence over Phenomenon: From Schleiermacher, we could see the primacy of the essence of human being over dignity. It is His ideality that enables Christ to have an

---

[158] Niebuhr, *Schleiermacher on Christ …*, pp. 212-213.

[159] Niebuhr, *Schleiermacher on Christ …*, p. 214.

[160] Schleiermacher, *The Christian Faith …*, p. 400.

[161] Schleiermacher, *The Christian Faith …*, p. 402.

[162] Niebuhr, *Schleiermacher on Christ …*, p. 215.

exemplary dignity. In Schleiermacher we could see human feeling as the capacity to have self consciousness. This self consciousness of human being could be seen as human capacity to transcend oneself in order to interact and influence each other. It is feeling that makes human being distinct from other animals even though their distinction is not their higher dignity but their potency of becoming.

2.9.2. The Dominance of (human) Spirit over the Flesh: In relation to the primacy of essence we could observe, from Schleiermacher, the dominance of the spirit over the flesh which can also be understood as the centrality of consciousness in humanity. He talks about sin and grace in terms of sin consciousness and grace consciousness. This is to say sin and grace are rooted in the feeling as he even says that "so long as there is no consciousness of sin there is no sin." Human essential nature is the inner being which functions as the centre of life. Renewal or change of human being happens in the inner being.

2.9.3. Sin as Feeling of Independence: The concept of Sin and Grace, in Schleiermacher, cannot be understood in terms of our relation to God but it is a condition of human being. Sin is not violation of God's commandment as such; it is a feeling of independence from God and identifying the self with the body. However, this feeling of independence needs to be considered in the horizontal relationship which must be feeling of independence from community or negation of the interconnectedness of human being. Human being is a being in a community and life is a corporate experience. Sin itself is never an individual affair and cannot be fully understood in isolation. This means that self consciousness is never independent rather is a community construct. In this view point, sin could be understood in terms of forces that stabilize a personal feeling unable to pursue his/her feeling of dependence.

2.9.4. Renewal of Humanity through Corporate Life and Fellowship: Schleiermacher understands human condition needs renewal for it has been feeble, repressed and unable to follow the feeling for goodness. For him, there can be a renewal of humanity in the life of fellowship and through corporate action that humanity can be strengthened for chasing goodness in life. This happens through stimulation by giving example to each other and motivating one another. On the other hand, whether it is a renewal or restoration is questionable for human horizon is futuristic in a historical process. In our attempt to formulate cross cultural theological understanding of humanity, we would like to argue for the empowerment of a person for the fuller realization of humanity in the future.

2.9.5. Person Forming and Culture Forming in a Community: For Schleiermacher, the horizontal establishment of a community is the result of love which is communicated through entering into fellowship. When love is communicated to a person, that person is enabled to communicate that love and that communication of love happens inside a community where love is existing in it. In this understanding of mutual influence in a community, we have person-forming activity which is also considered to be culture-forming activity. Everyone living in a particular community is having a particular culture through mutual engagement within that community.

2.10. Critical Evaluation:

2.10.1. The Historicity of Christ: Bultmann is critical of Schleiermacher's emphasis on Christ's historicity for it tends to limit in recovering Jesus' historical biography. Jon sobrino explains that the gospel narratives present Jesus by telling the story but this "historicization remains at the service of faith."[163] It is, therefore, necessary to know the importance of the story of the past with an acknowledgement that the stories that had been preserved are the product of faith and belief. It is always important to see Christ living and ongoing participation in the historical process.

2.10.2. Human Becoming Christ: Richard Niebuhr comments on Schleiermacher's theology as 'Christo-morphic' when he talks about Jesus of Nazareth as the ideal and measure of human nature.[164] However, this consideration of Schleiermacher's theology raises questions about whether human becoming Christ could be the negation of human identity and implicitly a negation of Christ's

[163] Jon Sobrino, *Jesus in Latin America* (Maryknoll, New York: Orbis Books, 1987), p. 30.

[164] Niebuhr, *Schleiermacher on Christ* ..., pp. 212-213.

distinctive identity as well. Christ became human being in the person Jesus of Nazareth, who could be rightly called as human measure and the horizon of human being. However, to become Christ is to cease human being, for Christ transcends human being.

2.11. Conclusion:

In Schleiermacher's thought, understanding the true essence of religion involves understanding the true essence of human being. His works were culturally rooted in the intellectual, philosophical and spiritual world of his own time. One of his main basic methodological foundations is his understanding of 'dialectic or togetherness of opposites'. This dialectical approach is that which enabled him to work on the "ideality and exemplary dignity" of Christ. It is through this dialectical nature of Christ that we could observe Jesus Christ as true human being and image of Christ is the horizon of human becoming.

From Schleiermacher we draw certain insights. One important insight is the primacy of human essential nature over our human dignity. Another insight is the historicity of human being that enables us to realize the human becoming in the future. One of the most important insights we get is the human cultural dimension. It is through the corporate life that human being has been shaped and it is because of this corporate life that the understanding of our being is culturally rooted.

In sum, the analysis above highlights the importance of interacting with cultural backgrounds in order to engage humanity in a cross-cultural context. For our cross-cultural engagement we will be looking at Raimond Panikkar in the next chapter.

Chapter 3

'Fullness of Man' in the Christophany of Raimond Panikkar

3.1. Introduction:

The Christological formulation of Schleiermacher insists that the nature of human being is culturally rooted. We now turn to the cross-cultural interaction of humanity in the light of Raimond Panikkar, who is of different cultural background from Schleiermacher as well as engaged himself in a cross-cultural context.

A brief study on the life and work of Raimond Panikkar will focus on his personal cross-cultural background. This is important because his theological formulation is truly embedded in his cross-cultural life experiences. We will also be dealing with certain major themes that reflect his thought. Apart from many other important topics that Panikkar has dealt in his theological undertaking, we will be confined to his understanding of Christ. His understanding of Christ is the central theme of his theological formulation in pursuit of religious harmony. For him, dialogue between different religious traditions is possible on the ground of the Absolute reality, which is Christ, from whom everything comes forth and ends.

However, the central focus, in this chapter, will be Panikkar's understanding of Christophany reflecting on the true humanity in the light of Christic experience.

3.2. The Context:

As the 19th Century witnessed the emergence of Neo-Hinduism, the renascent Hindu leaders began to dialogue with the western culture, Christianity. A grappling with Christ, people like Raja Ram Mohan Roy, Keshub Chunder Sen and P. C. Mozoomdar reflected upon the Indian religious traditions.[165] Taking the Hindu religious system and cultural settings of India, western missionaries of both Catholic and protestant churches sought to interpret an indigenous Christian theology. K. M. Banerji tried to present Christ, employing the term from the Vedas, 'Prajapathi,' who creates the world and preserves it through self-sacrifice. Brahmabandhav Upadhyay, who joined the nationalist struggle, interpreted the Trinity from the Hindu thought form of the Ultimate as Sat-Chit-Ananda.[166] A. J. Appasamy followed the south Indian Hindu tradition of *Bhakti* while both Pandipeddi Chenchaiah and Vengal Chakkarai outlined a Christocentric theology for the renewal of the Church and the nation.[167] This inclusivist methodology has been taken up and developed in various ways be several contemporary Indian theologians like Stanley J. Samartha, John B. Chethimattam and D. S. Amalorpavadass.[168] In this context, Raymond Panikkar understands theology as a dialogue where God's *logos* is interacting with ours. He says that

Theology is not gossip but dialogue. The '*logos*' of theology is not so much our logos as God's logos in interaction with our own. We have here not primarily and objective genitive but a subjective

---

[165] M. M. Thomas and P. T. Thomas, *Towards Indian Christian Theology* (Thiruvalla: The New Day Publications of India, 1992), p. 3.

[166] Thomas, *Towards Indian Christian Theology* ..., pp. 5-6.

[167] Kuncheria Pathil, *Trends in Indian Theology* (Bangalore: Asian Trading Corporation, 2005), p. 31.

[168] Pathil, *Trends in Indian Theology* ..., p. 32.

one. Theologizing is the listening to this word of God. … We have to listen, decipher, understand and finally realize those words.[169]

Jacob Parappally comments that the Christological reflection of Panikkar's time is dialogue and encounter between Hinduism and Christianity. The Christian claim of God's Mystery revealed for the whole world is challenged by Hinduism considering the equality of all religions.[170]

3.3. Panikkar's Life and Work:

Raymond Panikkar was born in Spain in 1918. His Hindu father and a Spanish Roman Catholic mother provided him the dual environment of both Christianity and Hinduism. He learned the Vedanta with the Bible and studied in Spain, Germany and Italy.[171] He earned his doctorate degree in chemistry, philosophy and theology. He became a consecrated priest in 1946. By the river of Ganges, he settled down in a small temple completely dedicating himself to study, prayer, meditation and writing. He went to his bishop, once a month, in Varanasi. He received an invitation from the Harvard University (USA) to be visiting professor. Panikkar, with the advice of his bishop, accepted the invitation and from then on, spent four-five months in the United States and the rest of the year in India.[172]

Francis X. D'Sa says that to understand Panikkar's thought we need to take note of his context, from where his concepts and ideas were conceived: His experiences of the Christian and secular traditions of Europe, Hindu and Buddhist traditions of India, in various fields

---

[169] R. Panikkar, "Indian Theology: A Theological Mutation," in *Theologizing in India,* edited by Amaladoss, T. K. John and G. Gispert-Sauch (Bangalore: Theologica Publications in India, 1981), p. 23.

[170] Jacob Parappally, *Emerging Trends in Indian Christology* (Bangalore: IIS Publications, 1995), p. 108.

[171] Robin Boyd, *An Introduction to Indian Christian Theology* (Madras: The Christian Literature Society, 1969), p. 222.

[172] Julien Ries, "Presentation: Anthropologlical perspectives for the third mellienium," in Raimon Panikkar, *The Fulness of Man: A Christophany,* translated by Alfred DiLascia (New York: Orbis Books and Delhi: ISPCK, 2006), p. xi.

of science, philosophy, theology and religions.[173] Panikkar, in fact, finds that Hinduism is a kind of Christianity in potential, a kind of Christianity in seed. His profound statement "I 'left' as a Christian, I 'found' myself a Hindu and I 'return' a Buddhist, without having ceased to be a Christian,"[174] also clearly reflects his multicultural background.

Panikkar says that the inter-cultural dialogue is his own personal experience as an *intra* religious experience. He says that "My personal circumstances (biological, historical and biographical) led me to accept the risk of conversion without alienation, assumption without repudiation, synthesis or symbiosis without syncretism or eclecticism."[175]

Among the many works of Panikkar, *The Unknown Christ of Hinduism,* first published in 1964 and the revised and enlarged edition in 1981 is truly remarkable. Robin Boyd comments that Panikkar technically manages both Thomistic and Vedantic terminology, simultaneously. Taking his stand on texts like Acts 14:16-17, "He left not himself without witnesses" and Acts 17:23 "Whom therefore ye ignorantly worship, him declare I unto you," Panikkar asserts that Christ is present in Hinduism. Because, of the hidden presence of Christ in Hinduism millions of Hindus find means of salvation and union with God.[176] Apart from the *Unknown Christ of Hinduism*, we will be concentrating on his work on *A Fullness of Man: A Christophany,* which was published in 2006. This work is a reinterpretation of traditional Christology in order to present the image of Christ that the contemporary people are capable of believing in. It is a reflection upon Christ's manifestation in human consciousness.

---

[173] Francis X. D'Sa SJ, "The Notion of God," in *The Intercultural Challenge of Raimon Panikkar,* edited by Joseph Prabhu (Maryknoll, New York: Orbis Books, 1996), p. 26.

[174] R. Panikkar, *The Intrareligious Dialogue* (New York: Paulist Press, 1978), p. 2.

[175] Raimon Panikkar, "Philosophy as Life-Style," in *Philosophers on their Own Work* (Bern, Frankfurt, Los Angeles: Peter Lang, 1978), p. 201. Cited by D'Sa SJ, "The Notion of God" ..., p. 27.

[176] Boyd, *An Introduction* ..., p. 222.

3.4. His Thought:

To understand Panikkar correctly, we need to consider the following three important themes of his thought:

3.4.1. Mutual Fecundation: Giving importance to the intercultural dimension of reality Panikkar says that if Christian theology claims to be catholic, it needs to be relevant and ultimately meaningful for other cultures. Ultimate mystery of reality and meaning of life is understood and interpreted by each culture using a different language. However, there is a danger of stagnation for each culture if it is not ready to be fecundated by other cultures.[177] Panikkar says that the relationship between the two religious traditions, Christian and Hindu, "is not one of assimilation, or of antagonism, or of substitution (the latter under the misnomer of 'conversion'), but one of *mutual fecundation.*"[178]

Beverly J. Lanzetta says that one of the most creative contributions of Panikkar to cross cultural research is his focus on the 'mutual fecundation or *perichoresis.*'[179] Panikkar, in *The Silence of God: The Answer of the Buddha* (1989), says that

Every being is what it is precisely because it is itself an ensemble of relationships and enters into intimate, constitutive relationship with other beings. And this relationship is such that it forms a radical unity that does not render things uniform, but, on the contrary, permits them to be diverse. Unity, then, and not the contrary, is the fundamental fact. This radical unity of relativity is intimate to each things, and yet at the same time it is transcendent, inasmuch as no thing really exhausts it, nor indeed all things together.[180]

---

[177] Raimond Panikkar, "The Theological Challenge of the 21st Century: The Harmony Among Religions," in *Indian Theology Seeking New Horizons,* edited by Kuncheria Pathil and Mathew Paikada (Mumbai: St. Pauls, 2007), p. 132.

[178] Raimundo Panikkar, *The Unknown Christ of Hinduism,* revised and enlarged edition (Bangalore: ATC, 1982), p. 12.

[179] Beverly L. Lanzetta, "The Mystical Basis of Panikkar's Thought," in *The Intercultural Challenge of Raimon Panikkar* ..., p. 91.

[180] Raimundo Panikkar, *The Silence of God: The Answer of the Buddha*, translated by Robert R. Barr (Maryknoll, New York: Orbis Books, 1989), p. 140.

Here, Lanzetta comments that Panikkar sees the dynamic, mystical perspective on the mutual reciprocity of unity and diversity, as constitutive of the building up of reality.[181]

3.4.2. Diatopical Hermeneutics: To communicate cross-culturally Panikkar develops diatopical hermeneutics which is based on *dialogical dialogue.*[182] This diatopical hermeneutics is not merely "morphological" and "diachronical" hermeneutics, it is

Diatopical hermeneutics stands for the thematic consideration of understanding the other without assuming that the other has the same basic self-understanding and understanding as I have. The ultimate human horizon, and not only differing contexts, is at stake here. The method in this third moment is a peculiar *dialogical dialogue, the dia-logos* piercing the *logos* in order to reach that dialogical, translogical realm of the heart (according to most traditions), allowing for the emergence of a myth in which we may commune, and which will ultimately allow understanding (standing under the same horizon of intelligibility).[183]

To Panikkar, this diatopical hermeneutics' base is experiential and cannot just be a matter of intellectual interpretation. We participate in the same Mythos[184] and we have deeper communion between "us" and "them" and the result is a "we."[185]

3.4.3. Theandrism and Cosmotheandrism: Panikkar's usage of two terms, 'theandrism' and 'cosmotheandrism,' is the expression of his understanding of reality and by which he sees the interconnectedness of all religions, all cultures and traditions.

---

[181] Lanzetta, "The Mystical Basis of Panikkar's Thought," ..., p. 92.

[182] D'Sa SJ, "The Notion of God," ..., p. 29.

[183] Raymond Panikkar, *Myth Faith and Hermeneutics: Cross Cultural Studies* (New York: Paulist Press, 1979), p. 9

[184] "Mythos is an important ingredient of Panikkar's understanding of consciousness. His contention is that consciousness can be neither simply identified with nor exhausted by the Logos. ("Witness and dialogue," 238-39) Mythos is as much and as important a characteristic of consciousness as Logos. Logos is the foreground, the expression, the thought, and Mythos is the background, the horizon, the unthought. ("The philosophical tradition," 345)." See D'Sa SJ, "The Notion of God," ..., p. 29.

[185] D'Sa SJ, "The Notion of God," ..., p. 29.

3.4.3.1. *Theandrism*: Panikkar gives importance to the inner core of religiosity in inter-religious encounter. In *The Trinity and World Religions* (1970), he classifies all human spiritualities in world religions broadly into three *margas* of Hinduism: the *karma* (action), the *bhakti* (love) and the *jnana* (knowledge). He shows the inter-relatedness of the three *margas* responding to Divine Reality as presented in the Trinity: Father, Son and Holy Spirit. However, Panikkar uses the term *theadrism* as an alternative term of trinity. He explains that "Theadrism is the classical and traditional term for that intimate and complete unity which is realized in Christ, between the divine and the human and which is the goal towards which everything here below tends in Christ and the Spirit."[186] In making an attempt to connect Buddhism, Christianity, Judaism, Islam and Hinduism, Panikkar tries to show that the Trinitarian understanding is not the monopoly of Christianity and different traditions contribute to deepen and transform all of them.[187]

3.4.3.2. *Cosmotheandrism*: Panikkar says that in the cosmotheandric principle, there are three irreducible dimensions which constitute the real, such as the divine, the human and the earthly.[188] He says that "There is a kind of perichoresis, 'dwelling within one another,' of these three dimensions of Reality, the Divine, the Human and the Cosmic – the I, the you and the it."[189] In the cosmotheandric reality, each being is in 'ontonomic' order where there is neither higher nor lower, but interdependence and interconnectedness. In cosmotheandrism, there is no distinction between secular and sacred, because secular is sacred and sacred is secular. There is no separation of time and eternity, but only

---

[186] Raymond Panikkar, *The Trinity and World Religions* (Madras: CLS, 1970), p. 69.

[187] Joseph Prabhu, "Lost in Translation," in *The Intercultural Challenge of Raimon Panikkar* ..., p. 7.

[188] Raimon Panikkar, "Colligite Fragmenta: For an Integration of Reality," in *From Alienation to At-Oneness,* edited by F. A. Eigo (Villanova, Pa.: Villanova University Press, 1977), pp. 73-74.

[189] Raimundo Panikkar, "The Myth of Pluralism: The Tower of Babel – A meditation on Non-violence," in *Cross Currents,* 29, no. 2. Sum, 1979: p. 217

tempiternity. Cosmotheandrism implies that Reality is a network of relationships, which Panikkar calls "radical relativity."[190]

The cosmotheandric intuition can be simply stated as the divine, the human and the earthly. They are the three irreducible dimensions which constitute the real and this triune constitution is presented by everything that exists. This does not mean that everything is directly or indirectly related to everything else but this relationship is constitutive of the whole. "The cosmotheandric intuition is not a tripartite division among beings, but an insight into the threefold core of all that is, insofar as it is."[191]

3.5. Understanding of Christ:

Raimond Panikkar's understanding of Christ dominates his whole theology as his reflection on Christ is the main centre of his theology. We will discuss some of the important themes given to Christology:

3.5.1. Use of the Term 'Christ:' Panikkar states that the term 'Christ' is an ambiguous term. It could be either Greek translation of the Hebrew Messiah or the name given to Jesus of Nazareth. However, he does not propose using the term 'Christ' in a polemic or apologetic manner, but decides to continue using it as he says "for I believe it is important that the figure of Christ should regain its complete fullness of meaning..."[192] In *The Unknown Christ of Hinduism,* Panikkar explains that he uses the name 'Christ,' not Rama or any other name, for he thinks that it is a historical name and "still is one of the most powerful symbols of humankind, though ambivalent and much-discussed."[193]

3.5.2. Mystical Christ: Panikkar is seeking a living presence of the Mystery, which Christians call Christ, in other religious contexts and called by other names. The ambiguity of this living presence is the

---

[190] D'Sa SJ, "The Notion of God," ..., pp. 36-37.

[191] Raimond Panikkar, "The Cosmotheandric Intuition," *Jeevadhara,* 14 (January, 1984): p. 29.

[192] Raimon Panikkar, *Trinity and Religious Experience of Man* (Maryknoll, N. Y.: Orbis Books; London: Darton, Longman and Todd, 1973), p. 53. Cited by D'Sa SJ, "The Notion of God," ..., p. 37.

[193] Raimundo Panikkar, *The Unknown Christ of Hinduism,* revised and enlarged edition (Bangalore: ATC, 1982), pp. 26-27.

depth of the Mystery as well as the human inability to comprehend or identify the Mystery.[194] Panikkar says that the unknown reality is "which Christians call Christ, discovered in the heart of Hinduism, not as a stranger to it, but as its very principle of life."[195] The main thesis of his book on *The Unknown Christ of Hinduism* is that the Christian belief in Christ as symbol of Life and Ultimate Truth is the same with the Mystery, to which every human being is attracted in order to overcome present condition. The Mystery is called by many names and is experienced in many forms and "it can be called neither one nor many."[196] It is important to note that though Christ is the Mystery, but that Mystery cannot be totally identified with Christ.[197] Panikkar explains that the title is not *The Hidden Christ,* which could mean the secret known to the Christians but not to the Hindus. He, therefore, puts stress on "the Presence of the one Mystery (not necessarily the 'same' Mystery) in both traditions." The Mystery is not a "purely transcendent divine reality" but equally immanent, which "possesses a historical dynamism."[198]

3.5.3. Christ as the Source of Reality: Robin Boyd says that the fundamental text of Hinduism, the Brahma Sutra (1:1, 2), which reads *Janmadi asya yatah*,[199] has been interpreted in a variety of ways by different interpreters like Sankara, Ramanuja, etc.[200] One major problem seen in Sankara is that if Brahman is the Absolute, how can the absolute cause the world? Sankara's followers said that Brahman is not the cause of the world but is Isvara.[201] However, Panikkar interprets the text and says that

That from which all things proceed and to which all things return and by which all things are (sustained in their being) is God, but we

---

[194] Gerald T. Carney, "Christophany: The Christic Principle and Pluralism," in *The Intercultural Challenge of Raimon Panikkar* ..., p. 135.

[195] Panikkar, *The Unknown Christ* ..., p. 20.

[196] Panikkar, *The Unknown Christ* ..., p. 23.

[197] Panikkar, *The Unknown Christ* ..., p. 24.

[198] Panikkar, *The Unknown Christ* ..., p. 26.

[199] *Janmadi asya yatah* means that "Brahman is the total ultimate cause of the world." See Boyd, *An Introduction* ..., p. 223.

[200] Boyd, *An Introduction* ..., p. 223.

[201] Boyd, *An Introduction* ..., p. 112.

detect two 'moments' in it: the 'first' is the invisible origin whence the source springs forth; the 'second' *is primo et per se* not a silent Godhead, an inaccessible Brahman, not even God the Father, source of all Divinity, but in a very true sense Isvara, God the Son, the Logos, the Christ.[202]

He explains that 'that' of the text is not a Platonic demiurge,[203] a secondary divinity, it is God, the Absolute, the source and ultimate reality. However it is distinct because it is its expression, image and revealer. This 'that' is a divine Person 'begotten' by God, equal in nature, yet distinct in personality.[204] Panikkar clearly states that "Christ stands for that center of reality, that crystallization-point around which the human, the divine and the material can grow. Rama may be another such name, or Krishna, or (as I maintain) Isvara, or Purusha, or even Humanity."[205]

3.5.4. Christ as the Ground of Encounter: Panikkar, in his book *The Unknown Christ of Hinduism,* presents Christ as the ground of encounter of all religions. He finds that doctrinal parallelism and cultural synthesis are inadequate as meeting points. He says that it is not possible to have a living encounter by simply pointing out similarities or common features on the practical or theoretical levels.[206] He even believes that doctrinal comparison can never form the ultimate basis for the integral encounter between living religions like Christianity and Hinduism.[207] He says that there are two premises of dialogue: first is the "basic tenets out of which the doctrines have been developed," and second is the "reality, the *existential truth*

---

[202] Panikkar, *The Unknown Christ ...*, pp. 155-156.

[203] *Platonic Demiurge*: Plato in the *Timaeus,* myth of the creation of the world, spoke poetically of the Creator as a craftsman. The Greek word 'demiourgos' passed into Christian usage as the equivalent of 'Creator'. It fell into disrepute for having been adopted by the Gnostics as the designation of the inferior deity who had made the world badly. See Alan Richardson, "Demiurge," in *A Dictionary of Christian Theology,* edited by Alan Richardson (Philadelphia: The Westminster Press, 1960), p. 90.

[204] Panikkar, *The Unknown Christ ...*, p. 156.

[205] Panikkar, *The Unknown Christ ...*, p. 27.

[206] Panikkar, *The Unknown Christ ...*, p. 38.

[207] Panikkar, *The Unknown Christ ...*, p. 39.

which the doctrines try to explain." In both of these dimensions, the doctrinal sphere is transcended and more room is there at the level of dialogue than a mere doctrinal discussion.[208] He even says that the cultural synthesis is inadequate for an in-depth encounter between Hinduism and Christianity for it cannot take place on the profane level of a merely cultural relationship.[209]

3.5.4.1. *The Hindu ground of encounter*: Panikkar says that Hinduism, within its structure, has room even for Christianity though their ideas do not coincide.[210] Generally, Hindus welcome Christianity as a younger sister of another religion for they are convinced that all religions are good so far as they lead human being to perfection.[211] A more recent form of Hinduism tends to a kind of syncretism which is characteristically Hindu type. This Neo-Hinduism says we should renounce what separates us, diminish our freedom and expansion of being.[212] We meet in the Absolute alone at the end of our pilgrimage where we encounter one another. There is no meeting point in differences but we shall meet only in what unites us giving up what makes us different.[213]

3.5.4.2. *The Christian ground of encounter*: According to Panikkar, both Hinduism and Christianity believe in God does not mean that they meet in their respective conceptions of God, but in God, the Absolute, the Ultimate. The meeting point which is a transcendent platform can be the end and goal but not the starting point. Therefore, we need a meeting place which is more than an idea or a concept, more than just humanity with its material needs.[214] Panikkar, therefore, says, "This, then, is Christ: that reality from whom everything has come, in whom everything subsists, to whom everything that suffers the wear and tear of time shall return. He is the embodiment of Divine Grace who leads everyone to God."[215]

---

[208] Panikkar, *The Unknown Christ* ..., p. 40.

[209] Panikkar, *The Unknown Christ* ..., p. 40.

[210] Panikkar, *The Unknown Christ* ..., p. 45.

[211] Panikkar, *The Unknown Christ* ..., p. 46.

[212] Panikkar, *The Unknown Christ* ..., p. 47.

[213] Panikkar, *The Unknown Christ* ..., p. 48.

[214] Panikkar, *The Unknown Christ* ..., p. 48.

[215] Panikkar, *The Unknown Christ* ..., p. 49.

From this point of view, Christ is already in Hinduism, in their prayer and in their form of worship. Christians and Hindus can no longer claim truth as their possession rather possessed by truth. The Christ has not yet completed his mission either in Christianity or in Hinduism. Both Christians and Hindus, therefore, meet "in the depths of death which is renunciation of ourselves – including our long-held opinions of other – and in the acceptance of 'new life' which is always there at the heart of true religion."[216]

3.5.5. Christ of Theandrism: In *The Unknown Christ of Hinduism,* Panikkar says that 'Within the Christian tradition this Christ is incomprehensible without the Trinity. A non-Trinitarian god cannot become incarnate. A non-Trinitarian Christ cannot be totally human and totally divine."[217] In his book *The Trinity and World Religions* (1970), Panikkar says that the Son in the Trinity is God, the divine person, the Lord, the one who acts, who creates and through him everything was made. Everything exists in him and is the beginning and the end. Therefore the Son is the Mystery hidden since the world began, which the scriptures speak and which, for Christians, was manifested in Christ.[218] In this theandrism, Panikkar argues, against Nestorianism[219] and monophysism,[220] that Christ is both God and human at one and same time. Christ is Jesus, Christ is God and is the Son of the Father and his Spirit is the Holy Spirit. To envisage in separation from one another would destroy the whole mystery which is the transcendence of the mystery of the

[216] Panikkar, *The Unknown Christ* ..., pp. 49-50.

[217] Panikkar, *The Unknown Christ* ..., p. 28.

[218] Panikkar, *The Trinity and World Religions* ..., pp. 50-51.

[219] *Nestorianism*: A theological norm set by Theodore of Mopsuestia (ca. 350-428) provided authoritiative biblical exegesis. Nestorian Christology, in the adoptionist trend of Antioch, called Mary as the 'Christ-bearer' rather than the 'God-bearer.' It believed that that the Logos merely dwelt in Jesus but did not deify him. Though the Council of Ephesus in 431 condemned Nestorius, the teaching went as the Chalcedon (451) failed to bring peace. See Wolfgang Hage, "Nestorians," in *The Encyclopedia of Christianity* ..., p. 722.

[220] *Monophysism*: It is a movement against the Council of Chalcedon, in the fifth Century, that view Christ as having one divine nature, not two, after the incarnation. This movement became a potent force in the Eastern theology and politics. See J. Rebecca Lyman, "Monophysites," in *The Encyclopedia of Christianity*..., p. 637.

Father, immanence and fullness of the mystery of the Spirit and the homogeneity to human of the personal mystery of Christ.[221]

3.5.6. The Cosmotheandric Christ: Panikkar's Christ is a symbol of the cosmotheandric Reality as he says

Christ is still a living symbol for the totality of reality: human, divine and cosmic. Most of the apparently more neutral symbols such as God, Spirit, Truth and the like truncate reality and limit the center of life to a discriminate principle, a non-historical epiphany, and often an abstraction.[222]

Jyri Komulainen says that Panikkar, in his earlier work, suggested that the convergence of religions could be realized in theandrism. After his pluralistic turn, he continues to describes Christ using terms such as 'link', 'mediator' and also 'conveyer' and puts Christ on a cosmic horizon.[223]

Christ, manifest or hidden, is the only way to God. Even by definition the unique link between the created and the uncreated, the relative and the Absolute, the temporal and the eternal, earth and heaven is Christ, the only mediator. Between these two poles everything that functions as intermediary, link, 'conveyer', is Christ, the sole priest of the cosmic priesthood, Ruler of the Universe par excellence.[224]

Here, Panikkar has broadened his christic principle to embrace, without exception, the totality of being, reality as a whole.[225] According to this recent Christological thinking, Christ is the symbol that symbolizes nothing less than reality itself. As such, Christ cannot be only theandric, but is more extensively cosmotheandric. Panikkar, in *A Dwelling Place for Wisdom* (1993), elaborates the cosmotheandric Christ as follows:

The mystery which is the beginning and will be the end; the Alpha and the Omega through which everything comes into being;

---

221 Panikkar, *The Trinity and World Religions* ..., p. 70.

222 Panikkar, *The Unknown Christ* ..., p. 27.

223 Jyri Komulainen, *An Emerging Cosmotheandric Religion? Raimon Panikkar's Pluralitic Theology of Religions* (Helsinki: University of Helsinki, 2003), pp. 118-119.

224 Panikkar, *The Trinity and World Religions* ..., p. 52.

225 Komulainen, *An Emerging Cosmotheandric Religion?* ..., p. 120.

> the light shining upon all creatures; the word contained in every authentic work; reality entirely material, completely human, and simply divine yet everywhere at work and unreachably present wherever reality exists; the meeting place at the crossroads of reality where all kingdoms meet; that which does not come with trumpet sounds and which one should not regard as being here or there; that of which we are not aware when acting in good or bad ways and which is still "right there;" that which we are –and are supposed to be –and which we have been; this symbol of all reality, not just as it used to be or is now but also as it will continue to be freely, even through our cooperation; that mystery, I believe, is Christ.[226]

From the above quotation we see clearly that Panikkar's Christ is the mystery which is the beginning and the end, the source of all being, who has a cosmic horizon, who is reality entirely material, who has human and divine nature, who is at work everywhere and who is the meeting place of all reality.

3.6. From Christology to Christophany: 'The Fulness of Man':

Gerald T. Carney says that Panikkar expands the dimensions of Christ, not only as savior and revealer but as the Mystery, the constitutive principle, the creative source of the Reality in which all participate. He says that "the unfolding of the Mystery of Christ as christic principle, in each person and in the world, as in the theological imagination, is a Christophany."[227]

Panikkar, in his work on *The Fullness of Man: A Christophany* (2006), is doing the work of deepening the classical Christology. He proposed a new discipline which he named Christophany with an intention to offer to the contemporary world a "response to the yearning for the fullness of life that burns in every heart."[228] Panikkar explains the task of Christophany as

> Christophany, simply intends to offer an image of Christ that all people are capable of believing in, especially those

---

[226] Raimon Panikkar, *A Dwelling Place for Wisdom,* translated by Annemarie S. Kidder (Delhi: Motilal Banarsidass, 1993), p. 153.

[227] Carney, "Christophany: The Christic Principle and Pluralism," ..., p. 131.

[228] Panikkar, *The Fulness of Man* ..., p. xxv.

> contemporaries who, while wishing to remain open and tolerant, think they have no need of either diluting their "Christianity" or of damaging their fidelity to Christ. And Christophany offers the same experience to all those who nourish an interest in that Man who lived some twenty centuries ago but still seems, to many people, to live.[229]

3.6.1. Meaning of Christophany: By Christophany, Panikkar means "a manifestation of Christ to human consciousness and includes both an experience of Christ as well as a critical reflection on that experience." It is not to abolish or ignore the traditional Christology for every growth requires both continuity and change. It does not replace but prolongs and deepens the unexplored and proposes new perspectives. In Christophany, unlike Christology, meeting with Christ is not reducible to a simple doctrine or intellectuality. He says that though the spirit is inseparable from the living Christ, it is not subordinated to Logos Christ. Therefore the word "christophany" appeals to the Spirit too.[230] Christophany includes both the figure of the historical past and the reality of the present. It is not merely exegesis of the text or archaeology, not even exclusive analysis or deductive reflection of historical reality for Christ does not belong to the past alone. It is open to a dialogue with other religions as well as the interpretation of the same tradition on the basis of a scenario that embraces the past and the present.[231]

3.6.2. 'The Christic Experience': Panikkar came up with his nine *sutra*[232] with an intention "to constitute a middle way between the classical theology, which inserts the figure of Christ in a

[229] Panikkar, *The Fulness of Man* ..., p. 9.

[230] Panikkar, *The Fulness of Man* ..., p. 10.

[231] Panikkar, *The Fulness of Man* ..., p. 11.

[232] Panikkar says that "I use the word *sutra* rather than thesis because the deductive method is not valid for the *sutra,* which speaks to us from within a level of consciousness that must already have been attained before we can grasp its meaning... These nine *sutra* are not theses to be defended. They are, rather, condensations of experiences lived (and often suffered) within the framework of tradition. They are "threads" that, along with others, form the texture of reality." See Raimon Panikkar, *The Fulness of Man: A Christophany,* translated by Alfred DiLascia (New York: Orbis Books and Delhi: ISPCK, 2006), p. 143.

monotheistic frame, more or less qualified, and a theoclastic current that wishes to "free" Christ (and Christianity) from every bond with "God."[233] Let us see the brief summary of the nine *sutra*:

3.6.2.1. '*Christ is the Christian Symbol for the whole of Reality*': Salvation is full realization or divinization (in traditional term) that occurs only in union with the divine, whose symbol in Christian language is Christ. To say Christ is "the symbol of the whole of reality" includes all the mysteries of human being as well as the universe. Christ "is not only the 'first-born' but the 'only begotten,' the symbol of reality itself, the cosmotheandric symbol par excellence."[234]

3.6.2.2. '*Christian recognizes Christ in and through Jesus*': The Council of Jerusalem, which abolished circumcision (Acts 15:1ff) did not supplant the Jewish Messiah but recognized Jesus in whom "the whole fullness of divinity lives corporeally" (Colossians 2:9). In Jesus "the mystery that has been kept secret" since the beginning has now revealed itself (Romans 16:25), and that "through him all things have been created" (Colossians 1:16).[235] However, Panikkar assures that "Jesus is Christ, but Christ cannot be identified completely with Jesus of Nazareth."[236]

3.6.2.3. '*The Identity of Christ is not the same as his Identification*': For Panikkar, identity and identification is not the same. Therefore, a contemporary reflection on Christ should neither be limited to the exegesis of texts nor contented with his identification. It must reflect Christ and seek the identity of Christ.[237] The discovered identity in a personal encounter must accept the criteria of identification and must seek to discover the identity which in turn confirms that the identification is correct.[238]

3.6.2.4. '*Christians do not have a monopoly on the knowledge of Christ*': No one can bring complete satisfaction to the human thirst for the infinite. The fact that Christians do not have full

---

233 Panikkar, *The Fulness of Man* ..., p. 143.

234 Panikkar, *The Fulness of Man* ..., p. 147.

235 Panikkar, *The Fulness of Man* ..., p. 149.

236 Panikkar, *The Fulness of Man* ..., p. 150.

237 Panikkar, *The Fulness of Man* ..., p. 154.

238 Panikkar, *The Fulness of Man* ..., p. 155.

knowledge of Christ means that they are not master of Christ and Christ transcends all understanding. What is needed is to explain how Christ is manifested in other religions. Though other religions do not speak of Christ they have different symbols to the one whose function is equivalent to the function of Christ.[239]

3.6.2.5. '*Christophany transcends Tribal and historical Christology*': Majority of scholars today agree that the God of the Hebrews was a tribal God. The task of Christians is conversion of a tribal Christology into a christophany which is less bound to a single cultural current. Christophany affirms that history is not the only dimension of the real and the reality of Christ is not exhausted with the historicity of Jesus.[240]

3.6.2.6. '*The protological, Historical, and Eschatological Christ Is a Unique and Selfsame Reality, Distended in time, Extended in Space, and Intentional in Us*': There are not three Christs–the creator, redeemer and glorifier. Since we find the full manifestion of Trinity in Christ, christophany makes sense only within a Trinitarian vision.[241] There is a threefold tension in our consciousness of reality. Firstly, we feel ourselves "distended in time," i.e. temporal and interval of time. Secondly, everything that exists is "extended in time," i.e. corporeal and parts. Thirdly, our "intentional nature" i.e. striving and purposeful. "Everything in us tends toward something more or something else."[242]

3.6.2.7. '*The Incarnation as Historical Event is also Inculturation*': Incarnation is a cultural event that is intelligible only within a particular religiocultural context of a specific history. The divine incarnation is not a historical event but a divine Trinitarian act. The only begotten is the first begotten and the incarnation is the total reality of the Logos.[243] Christophany not only seeks to interpret the historical facts of Jesus of Nazareth, it rather seeks to accept

[239] Panikkar, *The Fulness of Man* ..., p. 157.

[240] Panikkar, *The Fulness of Man* ..., p. 162.

[241] Panikkar, *The Fulness of Man* ..., p. 165.

[242] Panikkar, *The Fulness of Man* ..., pp. 166-167.

[243] Panikkar, *The Fulness of Man* ..., p. 170.

critically "the mystery that has appeared, been manifested, and now revealed" (Romans 16:26) by means of our human cognition.[244]

3.6.2.8. '***The church is Considered a Site of the Incarnation***': We are in the process of the full revelation of the children of God as long as the whole creation groans in pain of childbirth. This process occurs in the church which is also realized in the "visible church" despite all her human shadows and sins. The whole universe pulsates in the church until its final destiny. The role which Christophany shows us is the recapitulation of all things in Christ.[245]

3.6.2.9. '***Christophany is the Symbol of the Mysterium coniunctionis of Divine, Human, and Cosmic Reality***': As the cosmotheandric experience involves divine, human and world, the function of Christ is not limited to redeeming humanity alone but embraces restoration of the world.[246] "In Jesus Christ the finite and the infinite meet, the human and the divine are joined. In him the material and the spiritual are one, and also the male and the female, high and low, heaven and earth, the historical and the transhistorical, time and eternity."[247]

3.7. Humanity in the Light of Christic Experience:

Looking at the Christic Experience, let us draw some insights to understand what it means to be a human being. Panikkar's understanding of human being is engaged with cross-cultural interaction and is not something like a doctrine that can be universalized to be relevant to all cultures. However, there are some important points which everyone may ponder and reflect upon it from various corners and find it helpful to be truly human being in different contexts.

3.7.1. Human Being as Mystical Being: The first important understanding of human being in Panikkar is about human condition that human being is a mystical being.[248] To say human being is a

[244] Panikkar, *The Fulness of Man* ..., p. 172.

[245] Panikkar, *The Fulness of Man* ..., p. 178.

[246] Panikkar, *The Fulness of Man* ..., p. 181.

[247] Panikkar, *The Fulness of Man* ..., p. 181.

[248] Panikkar, *The Fulness of Man* ..., p. 40.

mystical being is equivalent to say there is a mystery in human being. The horizon of human being is not limited to the realm of finite, but extended to the realm of infinite. Human being capable of mystical experience indicates human capacity to mediate and to dialogue.

3.7.2. Humanity is a Call forward (Vocation): Panikkar says that "Being' is a verb, a communitarian – that is, personalist – action."[249] This is to say that to be human being involves action and moving towards fullness of life. Human being is not just a being in stagnant, but has to move towards the goal through intuitive realization of human horizon in the interconnectedness of the whole being. Every human has vocation to live a life in fullness and to ignore this vocation is unbecoming evil. Moreover, everyone must be free to pursue that vocation and anything that cause hindrance to achieve that vocation is sin.

3.7.3. Universal Experience of Reality: One of the most important human horizons that we can draw from Panikkar is human horizon towards Reality. This is a horizon to participate in the ultimate reality. The Indian tradition has a cosmotheandric view towards the reality in which human being is one of the participants. Reality is revealed in each culture and tradition and everyone has the opportunity to experience the ultimate reality. Truth cannot be absolutized or limited to one tradition or culture for each culture constitutively participates in the realization of reality. There cannot be individualistic and exclusive claims that cause monoculture. There cannot be monopoly of truth for any culture because reality has been experienced in different places, times and situations. The experience of truth in a particular culture cannot exhaust reality and each experience needs to be seen as part of the truth in order to dialogue for realization of the reality.

3.7.4. The Cosmic Horizon of Human Being: From Panikkar we can see the human cosmic horizon which shows human incompleteness without cosmos. Human fullness is possible only with having dialogical relationship with other creation. Human being is one aspect of creation and participates in the constitutive reality, which is formed by the integral relationship between God-human-world. Panikkar says that human being is "neither a separate

[249] Panikkar, *The Fulness of Man* ..., p. 64.

"individual" nor a "person" in isolation from the rest of the universe, including the divine."[250] For the whole of reality is constitutively interconnected, human being is not a being in itself, but a being connected to the divine as well as creatures. Human being is formed of spirit, soul and body.[251] He uses the term 'cosmotheandric' to explain the nature of Reality which means that reality is constitutively formed by the radical relationship between God, human and world. This is the ground of possibility for human being to participate in the reality.

3.7.5. Self-transcendence as a Way of Life: For Panikkar, Christianity is not so much a religion in the context of religious pluralism. Christianness constistutes a radical openness to the activity of the Spirit, solidarity with others and incarnates itself in each environment to the extent of losing itself in bringing clarity and deeper vision to all. Christianity should not assert its own claims against others as another religion and play its role in socio-political activities that violate religious integrity. In his discussion on the Christic principle, Panikkar has contributed the task to develop Christianity as "a way of life, a Christianness that, having died to its own desire to exclude and dominate, can confront the powers of division and can participate in a shared meal of reconciliation."[252]

3.8. Critical Evaluation:

3.8.1. Divinization of Human Being: Panikkar understands human being as possessing a divine spark which is a spirit that makes human being able to become divine. That divine spark within us is a spirit, he says, "that makes us divinizable in a way that is very different from all other beings."[253] From this statement, we see that human being can become divine or participate in the divine being. Here, what does he mean by divinization? Is divinization a negation of humanity? We raise this question because when he talks about cosmotheandrism where we see the distinctions between the divine,

---

[250] Panikkar, *The Fulness of Man* ..., p. 68.

[251] Panikkar, *The Fulness of Man* ..., p. 68.

[252] Carney, "Christophany: The Christic Principle and Pluralism," ..., p. 142.

[253] Panikkar, *The Fulness of Man* ..., p. 68.

the human and the world. He says that "the entire cosmotheandric experience is implicit here – the divine, the human, and the world."[254] If divinity is something different from human being, what does human becoming divine mean? Is it human becoming God?

3.9. Conclusion:

Panikkar's theological formulation is influenced by his multi-cultural background. His encounter with different religious traditions motivated him to find a meeting place for all religions in which he thinks that reality is the only possible place where all religions can meet, that is Christ. Panikkar's main concern is that all religions are good and contributive in realizing the truth, which is reality. Each religion contains the Mystery whether they know it or not. Christians see that mystery in Jesus Christ but that does not mean that Christ is Jesus. He rather expands the dimension of Christ that it is not the exclusive property of Christianity but the source of Reality in which all participate. He develops the idea of Christophany in place of Christology, in which he does not negate the concept of Christology or historical Jesus but makes a new venture in finding the reality of Christ beyond Jesus.

Through our exploration of Panikkar's understanding of Christ, we observe Christ as the ground and destiny of humanity. It is Christ who had mystical experience and profound intuition in which everyone must participate. This participation in the Christ mystical experience is the horizon of human becoming. To put it differently, human horizon is towards Reality, which is the indwelling of divinity in human being.

From Panikkar, we get to affirm the cross-cultural resourcefulness in the realization of truth. Through the universal experience of the mystery in different cultural settings, he argues for the necessity of having dialogue to realize the constitutive nature of reality. It is our insight that we must see the interconnectedness of all beings and live a self-transcending life in this historical process of fuller realization of humanity.

---

[254] Panikkar, *The Fulness of Man* ..., p. 181.

Chapter 4

Constructing the Cross-Cultural Theological Anthropology

4.1. Introduction:

We have discussed Schleiermacher and Panikkar, focusing on their Christological interpretation, in the previous two chapters (II and III). We will now interact with both of them that will not be just a fusion of two horizons or correlation, but engaging ourselves in different cultural backgrounds that would help us realize the mystery of human being.

In constructing cross-cultural theological anthropology, we are seeking our foundation on Christology. This involves dealing with Christological issues and exploration of how 'image of Christ' can be the ground of understanding humanity. This chapter will engage some Christological issues that are involved in constructing a cross-cultural theological anthropology.

Observing the human horizon towards image of Christ in the light of Schleiermacher, we will interact with Panikkar's understanding of human horizon towards Christophany (the indwelling of divinity in human being or manifestation of Christ in human consciousness). Despite the differences in their spatial and temporal locations, both Schleiermacher and Panikkar argue for a religious rootedness within the very nature of human being, which is the primacy of essence over phenomenon. We will, therefore, look at their similar emphasis on the mystical experience that transforms human condition in the community consciousness and fuller humanity.

4.2. Christological Issues Involved in Cross-Cultural Theological Anthropology:

There are certain Christological issues involved in a cross-cultural interaction for the understanding of humanity.

4.2.1. The Dialectical Nature of Christ: Person and Work of Christ: The dialectical nature of Christ is the point where we ground our cross-cultural interaction. The dialectic of Christ's nature involves the relationship between the divinity and humanity, person and work, ontological and functional. Jon Sobrino clearly affirms the historical Jesus as his starting point instead of the Chalcedonian formula which presupposes a "descent."[255] However, we are dealing with the Chalcedonian formula of Christ's full divinity and full humanity in one person as our ground of reconciling the immanent and transcendent.

4.2.1.1. *Schleiermacher's dialectic*: John A. T. Robinson says that the distinctive presupposition of a twentieth century Christology is the insistence on Jesus being a genuine product of the process. Schleiermacher is the first example of this modern thinking.[256] Indeed Schleiermacher is focusing on the historical Jesus emphasizing on Christ humanity and through the work of Christ that we have redemption and salvation. However, Schleiermacher says that the dignity and activity of the Christ (Redeemer) imply each other, and are inseparable. Though there is a division of doctrines into two: the person of Christ and the work of Christ, their content is the same.[257] It is through his understanding of "co-inhering polarity/togetherness

---

[255] Jon Sobrino, *Christology at the Crossroads* (London: SCM Press Ltd, 1978), pp. 3-4.

[256] John A. T. Robinson, *The Human Face of God* (Philadelphia: Westminster Press, 1973), p. 42.

[257] Schleiermacher, *The Christian Faith* ..., p. 376.

of opposites"[258] that Schleiermacher sees the dialectical nature of Christ.

4.2.1.2. *Panikkar's synthesis*: Panikkar proposes a synthesis which is not arrived through a dialectical process but the holistic or mystical vision of reality which sees polarities as the characters of reality. He says that, in a dialectical law of thesis things are independent and exclusive while the holistic and mystical vision of reality sees all are interdependent and mutually inclusive.[259] To overcome the dilemma of monism and dualism, Panikkar proposes the 'advaitic intuition' which is the immediate experience of the reality not absolutizing the difference or ignoring it. It expresses the tension between polarities and radical relativity of unity and differences.[260] In this thought Eternity and temporality are correlated in which time is experienced as constitutive of Being. It is not now is temporal and later as eternal but it is tempiternal[261] where there is the experience of the present as past in potency and future in hope.[262] Here History is neither absolutized nor neglected and this is important in understanding the mystery of Christ which is both the historical Jesus and the living Christ of existential experience.[263]

In our discussion on cross-cultural theological anthropology, we, therefore, may use the term 'dialectical' but not as a fusion of two horizons, rather as the constitutive and integral relatedness of something which we regard it as polar or opposite.

4.2.2. Christ as the Divine Person: In both Schleiermacher and Panikkar we have Christ as having human nature but with higher personality, that is divine personality. This divine personality in Christ has been understood by Schleiermacher as Jesus' constant

---

[258] Already discussed in Chapter Two (2.5.2.1).

[259] R. Panikkar, "The Silence of the Word: Non-dualistic Polarities," in *Cross Currents,* 24, no. 2-3, Sum-Fall (1974): p. 163.

[260] Parappally, *Emerging Trends* ..., pp. 113-114.

[261] Tempiternity according to Panikkar is "neither eternity (an objectified notion belonging exclusively to God), nor temporality (a much too subjective concept and the monopoly of the human being)." See Raimundo Panikkar, *Worship and Secular Man* (London: Darton, Longman and Todd Ltd., 1973), pp. 44-45.

[262] Panikkar, *Worship and Secular Man* ..., p. 45.

[263] Parappally, *Emerging Trends* ..., p. 114.

potency of God consciousness (His ideality), which distinguishes Jesus, though a historical individual, from all other human being. It is this divine personality (ideality) that enables Christ to communicate with human being.[264] Robinson says that, for Schleiermacher, Jesus environmental conditioning was limited to the manner of his life-style but there is inner 'unchangeable entity' which was not really affected by his experiences.[265]

Panikkar asserts that the term Person cannot be used in the Trinity as real analogy, because we can speak of God as a Person only in the case of the Son. The term, person, in its eminent and analogical sense, can be applied only to the Son.[266] Panikkar says that "It is the Son who acts, who creates. Through him everything was made. In him everything exists. He is the beginning and the end, the *Alpha* and the *Omega*. It is the Son, properly speaking – the Son manifested in Christ – who is the Divine Person, the Lord."[267]

4.2.3. Christ as the Mediator and Link: It is the divine personality that makes possible of relationship between the created and the uncreated, the relative and the absolute, temporal and eternal, earth and heaven. Christ, the divine person is the link, the only mediator between the finite and the infinite which various religious traditions name differently.[268] Panikkar says that "the son is the mediator, the *summus pontifex* (Great High Priest) of creation and also of the world. Beings *are* in so far as they participate in the Son, are *from, with* and *through* him. Every being is a *christophany* showing forth of Christ; it *is* only that."[269]

4.3. Image of Christ in Creation and Incarnation:

In our cross cultural interaction, we see Christ not only as the fullness but also the source of all creation (origin). We have incarnation as 'word became flesh,' from the Biblical tradition, which means that

---

264 Niebuhr, *Schleiermacher on Christ* ..., p. 226.

265 Robinson, *The Human Face* ..., p. 43.

266 Parappally, *Emerging Trends* ..., p. 129.

267 Panikkar, *The Trinity and World* ..., p. 50.

268 Panikkar, *The Trinity and World Religions* ..., p. 52.

269 Panikkar, *The Trinity and World Religions* ..., p. 53.

Christ is the fullness of all things. However, taking incarnation as 'materialization' or 'embodiment' or 'manifestation' of words, we could observe creation as the first incarnation, when Christ creatively incarnates the word in action. With this understanding of Christ as the source of all beings, let us see how image of God can be understood in term of image of Christ.

4.3.1. Image of Christ in Creation: Observing Christ/Logos, who is also God in the 'immanent trinity,'[270] as the Creator, we have the origin of all creation in Christ. For this reason, all the creations are bearing the image of Christ by way of likeness in the *trace*.[271] However, the distinct identity of human being as image of God is being a rational creature, having mind and intellectuality.[272] This image of Christ/God could be seen in term of potency of becoming, i.e. reason, intellectuality, self consciousness (Schleiermacher's term) and mystical or intuition (Panikkar's term). As Christ created human being, they are bearing a distinct image of Christ, who was to

---

[270] Christ is truly God in the immanent Trinitary of God. Moltmann says that the unique natures of the Father, Son and Spirit are determined through their relationships to one another. He began his explanation with the second definition in the Apostle's Creed that the Fatherhood of God is determined in respect of the Son. (See Jurgen Moltmann, *The Trinity and the Kingdom of God: The Doctrine of God* (London: SCM Press Ltd, 1981), pp. 163-167). Borrowing John Damascene's doctrine of the eternal *perichoresis* or *circumincessio* of the Trinitarian persons, Moltmann grasps the circulatory character of the eternal divine life. Through the exchange of energies the life process takes place in the triune God that the Father exists in the Son, the Son in the Father, and both of them in the Spirit, just as the Spirit exists in both the Father and the Son. Their unity lies in the circulation of life which they fulfill in their relations to one another. The perichoretic unity of the triune God is perceived and reflected in salvation history. (See Moltmann, *The Trinity* ..., pp. 172-178).

[271] Thomas Aquinas explains that there are two ways of understanding likeness. One is by way of *trace,* which is likeness by effects and imprints that all creation possess. The other one is likeness by *species,* which is 'image of God'possessed by rational creature in their mind that excels other non rational creature. See Thomas Aquinas, *The Summa Theologica,* Part I. QQ. LXXV – CII, translated by Fathers of the English Dominican Province (London: Burns Oates and Washbourne Ltd., 1920), p. 293.

[272] Aquinas, *The Summa Theologica* ..., p. 293.

incarnate. In this understanding of incarnation we could see creation as expansion of the divine being.

4.3.2. Image of Christ in Incarnation: We have economic trinity affecting the immanent trinity through the incarnation of Christ/ logos. That incarnation is self emptying (kenotic) and becoming a truly human being in the person Jesus Christ without losing his relation to God, that is divinity (Chalcedonian).[273] With this kenotic incarnation, the place of Christ in the immanent trinity is empty (Father – empty – Holy spirit). However, the horizon of the triune life of God has been opened to the Son or the incarnated one for which human being and the world (creation) could participate in the divine trinity by way of relationship but not diminishing the identity as being human and creation. In this sense, the term trinity may not necessarily indicate three, but a symbol of the interrelatedness of the divine being that encompasses God, The Son (Christ incarnation), Holy Spirit, human being and creation.

4.3.3. Image of Christ as the Permanent Identity of Human Being: Another important nature of incarnation that would be reflected through our cross cultural interaction is to understand incarnation as a permanent integration of God and human body.[274] This understanding of Christ incarnation as permanent is significant for our understanding of human identity as permanent. Christ, after resurrection was not becoming anything more than human being which indicates that human being is not becoming something else but fuller human being.

---

[273] Here, we draw our standpoint from the Chalcedonian formula which says Christ is "fully divine and fully human." For which we suggest the understanding of incarnation as Christ becoming fully human being by emptying Himself while maintaining His full divinity in terms of His relation to God.

[274] Drawing ideas from Pandippedi Chenchiah that incarnation is a perfected human body receiving the full divinity of God. Jesus ascended into Heaven but never resumed the place of second person in Trinity. "Humanity did not borrow Jesus to stay a while on earth. We have lent him to heaven to stay there for a while." See P. Chenchiah, "The Core: Fact of Jesus," *the Guardian*, 1947. Reproduced in D. A. Thangasamy, *The Theology of Chenchiah with Selections from His Writings* (Bangalore: CISRS, 1966), p. 80.

It is Panikkar's thought that realities are "not-two" but intimately related.[275] He argues that "the Absolute is not only transcendent but both transcendent and immanent all in one."[276] This is to solve the monistic and dualistic dilemma. "God and the world are neither one nor two."[277] This means that human being is differentiated from God (having particular identity) but intimately related to God. The divinity of human being is not the human-God, but human being in relation to God which concedes differentiation but not separation.

4.3.4. Eschatology: Divinization and Glorification: The future eschatological aspect of human being has been understood in terms of divinization, glorification, and reunification. Here is a very important point that needs to be made clear: this eschatological aspect should neither be deification nor christification, which is elimination of the distinct human identity. Panikkar says that "although we speak of divinization, we must observe that the moment we cease being men (sic), that divinization may turn into alienation."[278] As the light of our cross cultural interaction, divinization, therefore, should be understood in terms of the perfection of relationship with God and the attainment of dignity as a result of what has been gone through. It is very important to note that dignity is earned and achieved, while identity is inherent and cannot be removed.

Through our cross-cultural interaction, we affirm the primacy of identity over dignity which could be the ground of cross-cultural understanding of theological anthropology where God's culture and human culture are in dialogue.

4.4. Image of Christ as the Foundation of Cross-Cultural Theological Anthropology:

Drawing on insights from Schleiermacher and Panikkar, we will now try to formulate, having image of Christ as our foundation, the understanding of who human being is.

---

[275] Ewert H. Cousins, "Panikkar's Advaitic Trinitarianism," in *The Intercultural Challenge of Raimon Panikkar,* edited by Joseph Prabhu (Maryknoll, New York: Orbis Books, 1996), 120.

[276] Panikkar, *Trinity and World Religions* ..., p. 35.

[277] Panikkar, *Trinity and World Religions* ..., p. 35.

[278] Panikkar, *The Fullness of Man* ..., p. 138.

4.4.1. Christ as True Human Being: With our cross-cultural approach, we are seeking an affirmation of Christ as true human being by the following several points:

4.4.1.1. *Christ as completion of human nature*: For Schleiermacher "the appearance of Christ" is regarded as the completion of the creation of human nature.[279] Everything which Christ has brought into the life of human being is presented as a new creation. Christ, the Second Adam, is the beginner and originator of a more perfect human life and the completion of the creation of human being. This is a clear indication that it is not possible to attain higher life out of natural order which had its beginning in Adam.[280]

4.4.1.2. *Historicity of Christ*: Christ as the Second Adam is the indication that Christ is like all those who are descended from the first Adam, but has an absolutely potent God-consciousness. Christ enters the historical order of human nature and stands under the law of historical development, and then brings perfection through gradual expansion from the point at which He appears.[281]

4.4.1.3. *Christ as the source and vocation of full humanity*: When Panikkar explicates Christ as the source of reality, his Christ is bigger than the historical Jesus. However, this does not mean that Panikkar's Christ is bereft of historicity. Panikkar assures the historical Christophanic experience of the people in the person Jesus of Nazareth. When he said "Jesus is Christ, but Christ cannot be identified completely with Jesus of Nazareth,"[282] all divinity and fullness dwell in the person Jesus, but Jesus does not exhaust the whole being of Christ. Therefore, fullness of humanity originates in Christ and Christ is the destiny of human being.

4.4.2. Christ as the Origin of Human Being: Having our foundation on the image of Christ, we are seeking an understanding of human being as originally created in the image of Christ. Tertullian understood the image of God in terms of the image of Christ. He says that human being is the clay that put on the image of Christ, who was to be in the flesh. This could be possible for the Word also

[279] Schleiermacher, *The Christian Faith,* sec. 89 …, p. 366.

[280] Schleiermacher, *The Christian Faith* …, p. 367.

[281] Schleiermacher, *The Christian Faith* …, p. 367.

[282] Panikkar, *The Fulness of Man* …, p. 150.

is God, who being in the form of God thought it not robbery to be equal with God (Cf. Phil 2:6).[283] This is to say that Christ is truly God, in the immanent trinity, and human being, made in the image of God, is actually bearing the image of Christ.

This understanding of image of Christ may be settled with the Trinitarian framework as reflected in Panikkar's thought of the *theandrism*. In Panikkar's thought Christ is the symbol of reality from where everything proceeds and ends. He said that the whole of reality is nothing but God: Father, Christ and Holy Spirit. Christ is where all beings participate and find their place. They are fully what they are when they become one with Christ.[284] To Panikkar, Christ is not only at the end but also at the beginning. "He could not be the Omega of everything if he were not also the Alpha."[285] To Panikkar, Christ, in Christian tradition, is incomprehensible without the Trinity because a non-Trinitarian Christ cannot be totally human and totally divine.[286]

4.4.3. Image of Christ as the Horizon of Human Becoming: Schleiermacher speaks of Christ's 'exemplary dignity' and 'ideality' that Christ, like all other human being, is having human identity while distinguished from all others by the constant potency of His God-consciousness.[287] Here Christ ideality and exemplary dignity are seen as the human measure for they are in relation to human nature. Jesus Christ is seen as the ideal human being towards whom human being has to grow for He portrays the ideal and measure of human nature. Christ, as redeemer, is the one in whom "Adam" is finally formed.[288]

Panikkar asserts that "that from which the World comes forth and to which it returns and by which it is sustained, that is *Isvara*, the Christ."[289] Therefore, the full development and full realization of humanity is to participate in the whole of reality, Christ, who

---

[283] Tertullian, *Treatise on the Resurrection,* ..., p. 19.

[284] Panikkar, *The Unknown Christ* ..., p. 161.

[285] Panikkar, *The Unknown Christ of Hinduism* ..., p. 2.

[286] Panikkar, *The Unknown Christ* ..., pp. 27-28.

[287] Schleiermacher, *The Christian Faith,* sec. 93 and 94 ..., pp. 377-385.

[288] Niebuhr, *Schleiermacher on Christ* ..., pp. 212-213.

[289] Panikkar, *The Unknown Christ* ..., p. 162.

is the true nature and destiny of human being. Panikkar says that Christophany is a human horizon and Colossians 2:9 "For in him the whole fullness of divinity dwells bodily" is the human vocation.[290] This is to say that the dwelling of fullness of divinity in us is the horizon of human being. To Panikkar, Christophany is the manifestation of Christ to the consciousness of human being.[291] It is, therefore, as Francis D'Sa, S. J. comments, to experience Christ is to "re-live the mystical experience of Jesus Christ." It is to "participate in the same spiritual experience, the same profound intuition that Jesus Christ had."[292]

We, therefore, through our cross-cultural interaction, affirm the understanding of human being as bearing the image of Christ.

4.5. The Cross-Cultural Theological Anthropology:

After engaging with different cultural backgrounds of theological tradition we now have come to the understanding of human being in the cross-cultural context. Here we will discuss the nature of human being, the essence and identity of human being in the light of our cross cultural interaction.

4.5.1. Human Being as a Religious Being: Schleiermacher speaks of 'piety or religion' as a constitutive element of all human self consciousness which is neither knowing nor doing but a "determination of feeling or of the immediate self-consciousness."[293] Similarly, Panikkar also speaks about human being as capable of having mystical experience. In both the cases, we see human self-transcendency which both of them understood as the root of human religiosity. This could be the distinctive nature of human being in relation to animal which is reflected in what Ludwig Feuerbach says "religion has its basis in the essential difference between man and the brute – the brutes have no religion."[294]

---

[290] Panikkar, *The Fullness of Man* ..., p. xxvii.

[291] Panikkar, *The Fullness of Man* ..., p. 10.

[292] Francis D'Sa, S. J., "Forward: Fullness of "Man" or Fullness of "the Human"?" in Panikkar, *The Fullness of Man* ..., p. xxi.

[293] Niebuhr, *Schleiermacher on Christ* ..., pp. 174-175.

[294] Ludwig Feuerbach, *The Essence of Christianity*, translated by George Eliot (New York: Harper and Brothers Publishers, 1957), p. 1.

4.5.2. Human Being is a 'Person' of a Community: Niebuhr comments on Schleiermacher that the work of Jesus Christ as the second Adam is a "person-forming" work. Through the communication of his own life, Christ creates person and brings them into complete existence as human beings as having particular identities.[295] We have more explication of the meaning of 'person' in Panikkar that he understands human being as a person which is more than individual. For him, 'Person' is a 'mystery', which engross uniqueness and incomparability.[296] Human being cannot be understood in terms of individual but as a person, by his or her interaction in the society. Ted Peters says that "to be a person is more than just to be an individual. To be a person is to exhibit the truth of the whole of reality in, with, and under our individuality."[297] Understanding human being as a person involves having a particular identity or distinction from others but not in isolation. Human being is a 'person' who exists and participates in a community.

4.5.3. The Historical Consciousness as Human Becoming and Vocation: Leonardo Boff says that in the eighteenth century, there was a break-through of critical reason that enhanced historical studies.[298] Schleiermacher says that Christ's activity in the historical development is brought to perfection through gradual expansion.[299] Hans Georg Gadamer, with the influence of philosophy of Emmanuel Kant and Martin Heidegger understands history in terms of "classic"[300] which is reflected in Rudolf Bultmann's hermeneutical existential

---

[295] Niebuhr, *Schleiermacher on Christ* ..., p. 214.

[296] Panikkar, *Myth Faith* ..., p. 337.

[297] Peters, *God The World's Future* ..., p. 149.

[298] Leonardo Boff, *Jesus Christ Liberator* (Maryknoll, New York: Orbis Books, 1981), p. 2.

[299] Schleiermacher, *The Christian Faith* ..., p. 367.

[300] "When we call something classical, there is a consciousness of something enduring, of significance that cannot be lost and that is independent of all the circumstances of time - a kind of timeless present that is contemporaneous with every other present." See Hans Georg Gadamer, *Truth and Method* (London: Sheed and Ward, 1988), p. 288.

hermeneutics.[301] In reaction to existentialist theology, Pannenberg argues that theology makes sense only within the history that God shares with human being.[302] In Panikkar's *advaitic* intuition, we have tempiternity, which is neither eternity nor temporality.[303] He says that "the very consciousness of time implies that man (sic) has a certain platform outside that kind of time so as to enable him to be aware of it."[304]

In our cross-cultural approach, we affirm human being as a historical being that involves becoming in the historical process. Human being needs to find space and time for a meaningful and authentic existence. The historical consciousness takes seriously of the social and historical world and advocates involvement in the public life, politico-social world.

4.5.4. The Consciousness of Sin as Unbecoming: In the light of our discussion on human historical consciousness, we could see the nature of sin as human unbecoming. Schleiermacher, to avoid contradiction, offered a redefinition of original human perfection which allows the presence of sin. He regards original perfection as "predisposition to God-consciousness," which is an inner impulse that includes faculty of attaining God-consciousness by means of human organism, and the impulse to express that God-consciousness.[305] Here, perfection is not regarded as a fully developed and static human condition at the time of creation but a latent power of potentiality of human nature.[306] Therefore, human beings have the potential of becoming and anything that obstructs human becoming is to be considered as sin. Ted Peters says that "Sin and its fruit – evil – retard

---

[301] James C. Livingston, et al., *Modern Christian Thought,* vol. II, The Twentieth Century (New Jersey: Prentice Hall, 2000), pp. 349-352.

[302] Sobrino, *Christology at the Crossroads* ..., pp. 25-26.

[303] "The experience of the present, in fact, pierces, as it were the crust of the provisional and the flowing, not to fall onto a static intemporal bed, not to deny time, but to relish its kernel, so to speak. Any profound human experience occurs in time but not bound to or by time." See Panikkar, *Worship and Secular Man* ..., p. 45.

[304] Panikkar, *Worship and Secular Man* ..., p. 46.

[305] Schleiermacher, *The Christian Faith,* sec. 60 ..., p. 244.

[306] Niebuhr, *Schleiermacher on Christ* ..., p. 206.

this becoming. We sin by trying to fixate ourselves in present reality, thereby diverting or blocking God's call forward toward the new creation. Evil is unbecoming."[307]

4.5.5. Trinitarian Community as Human Ultimate Horizon: The community where human being participates is understood, with our cross-cultural approach, as the 'Trinitarian community' where everything is constitutively related to each other. The ultimate human horizon is, therefore, reflected in Panikkar's *cosmotheandric* principle, where we have three irreducible dimensions of Reality. He says, "there is a kind of perichoresis, 'dwelling within one another,' of these three dimensions of Reality, the Divine, the Human and the Cosmic – the I, the you and the it."[308] Looking at the image of Christ as the ground of all realities we understand two human horizons: cosmic horizon and divine horizon. These two horizons of human being are realized by participating in the Trinitarian community which brings fullness and completion of humanity.

4.6. Conclusion:

In our cross-cultural engagement with the understanding of human being we affirm the religiosity of human being, which means human being is a religious being. The religious problem is a human problem for religion is the highest value of human being, grounded in the very inner being of humanity. This is the common nature of human being. At the same time this common nature is not for universalism, which claims one absolute truth. In our cross-cultural interaction, we seek a particular identity in each individual, culture and tradition. For this purpose Christ is the centre whose image is not exhausted by any individual or particular culture or tradition. Every being has its own particular identity but finds fullness in the realization of the interconnectedness of the whole of reality. Truth is not just a fusion of dialectics but a constitutive of different traditions and cultures. Human being, uniquely created in the image of God that is represented in Christ's divine personality, participate in the divine community and that community consciousness leads us in forming a

---

307 Peters, *God The World's Future* ..., p. 147.

308 Panikkar, "The Myth of Pluralism: The Tower of Babel ..., p. 217.

community of relation where every individual is having a share both rights as well as responsibility.

Chapter 5

Conclusion
Humanity in the Cross-Cultural Theological Anthropology

5.1. Brief Summary:

For image of Christ has been envisioned, in Christian theology, as the horizon of human becoming, we have proposed, in the first chapter, the image of Christ to be the foundation of Christian theological anthropology. Looking at the development of Christian theological tradition and the arising contextual issues, we observe the importance of human studies and consider human subjectivity in theological undertakings. Observing a challenge for cross cultural interaction, we seek our foundation on Christology, where we find the meeting place of polarities: transcendence and immanence. With this Christological foundation we suggest 'image of Christ' as a hermeneutical device for understanding image of God. Image of God has been understood, traditionally, as the ground of human dignity. However, in our understanding of image of God in terms of representation, we conclude with the importance of claiming identity more than dignity, which suggest an understanding of human being having particular identity but not special dignity in a hierarchical structure of the whole cosmos.

Having Christology as our foundation for understanding human being, we explore, in the second chapter, Friedrich Schleiermacher's understanding of the person and work of Christ. Through our exploration, we find the primacy of the essence in human being. It is in the human essential nature where we find religion being rooted, which means religion as a particular human dimension. With his understanding of human self transcendency through consciousness, which he terms as 'feeling of dependence,' we see the merger between transcendence and immanence in the person Jesus Christ. That history becomes the horizon of human being. This understanding of togetherness of opposites (dialectic) has become the foundation of corporate life. This is a life in community which creates human personality and shapes culture. With this understanding of human cultural dimension we seek conversation partners of different cultural background in the third chapter.

Through our exploration of Panikkar's understanding of Christ, in the third chapter, we affirm the cross-cultural resourcefulness in the realization of truth. We see mystical experience as human potency of becoming. Panikkar, affirming the universal experience of the mystery in different cultural settings, argues for the necessity of having dialogue to realize the constitutive nature of reality. It is from here we seek to understand life in a historical process is to dialogue through self-transcendency for human becoming. We, therefore, make an attempt to construct a cross-cultural theological anthropology for better understanding of humanity.

Engaging those insights that we have drawn from both Schleiermacher and Panikkar, we make an attempt to formulate the cross-cultural understanding of human being in the fourth chapter. Considering the methodological issues that involve in our formulation, we interact with Schleiermacher's understanding of human horizon towards image of Christ and Panikkar's understanding of human horizon towards Christophany, which is indwelling of divinity in human being. Then we have come to realize human being as a religious being; human being as a being in a historical community and whose interaction inside a community is contributive of human becoming. It is at this situation that we make our venture, placing human being in the community of relationship as one particular participant among many, to find help in the realization of Truth.

Having this cross cultural approach we see that the claim of humanity is not just a retrieval of human identity or dignity from the past, but pressing on towards the fullness of human being that will be realized in the future. As we are dealing with the cross-cultural understanding of human being, our intention is not to produce a doctrine on humanity that would be relevant to all cultures, rather to observe how different cultures resourcefully reflect the mystery of life. In the light of our cross cultural interaction, let us see what it means to be human being in this historical process of becoming.

5.2. Humanity in the Cross-Cultural Context:

5.2.1. Humanity is Being in a Community: The first important aspect of human being that we observe through our cross-cultural interaction is that humanity is being in a community. This means that the mystery of humanity is realized and achieved through a corporate endeavor. Here we seek to understand being a human being itself is to engage in dialogue. This indicates that human being is incomplete without the existence of others. It is God's desire to create human being so that they will multiply and be many to fill the earth (Genesis 1:28). Panikkar says that human being cannot be understood in terms of individual but as a person by his or her interaction in the society.[309] We, therefore, affirm that life in fullness and completion is experienced only in the process of dialogue or relationship. Our human horizon, image of Christ, must be appearing into two realms:

5.2.1.1. *A community of human beings*: Human horizon extents to the whole community which is inclusive of all cultures, all religions and societies. A person must find fullness in a community where he/she can freely express oneself without diluting others. The best way to express this human horizon towards community is that an individual problem is a community problem and a community problem is an individual problem. It is, therefore, necessary to realize

[309] Panikkar, *Worship and Secular Man ...*, p. 5.

that we are participants in this community and we must actively participate in it. In such a situation, to live a life in isolation is a dehumanizing culture which could be conceived as the manifestation of human selfish desire.

5.2.1.2. *A cosmic community*: Human horizon is not limited to the human community alone; it rather extends to the cosmic horizon. The cross cultural approach seeks to dialogue with creation, without which there is no fullness of life in the community of the whole cosmos. This human cosmic horizon is inevitable to achieve fullness of life to the extent that human being becomes human being only in relation to other creation.

5.2.2. Self Acceptance as Empowerment: In our cross-cultural interaction, we are seeking the empowerment of a person to pursue for better humanity and to strife for fullness of life. One of the most important natures of human being is self consciousness, which is a distinctive nature of human culture from animal culture. Self consciousness is not just the knowledge about oneself, it is understanding oneself in relation to others, which involves comparison and examination of oneself. Self consciousness, though sounds individualistic, is possible only in the web of life. However, in the process of this self consciousness there could be two important moments that determine our search for true humanity.

5.2.2.1. *Self acceptance as wholeness of life*: The intuitive experience of a communion is expressed in a personal feeling for that feeling is determined by that community experience. Self acceptance is neither a pride in oneself nor a claim for individualistic life, but the result of the experience of acceptance inside a community. It is, therefore, the manifestation of the wholeness of life in a person that strengthens every individual to pursue for better realization of true humanity.

5.2.2.2. *Self denial as sin*: In relation to self acceptance, it is inevitable to see self denial as caused by corporate action. Self denial is an intuitive experience of a person that makes him/her deny the essential goodness within oneself. Any wrong conception about oneself, that is rejection of the essential goodness, causes self denial and a person who experiences that feeling cannot become or make out who he/she is.

When a person is caused to have negative conception about oneself, he/she is unable to become what he/she is supposed to be. James Cone says that liberation is knowledge of self; it is a vocation to affirm who I am created to be.[310] The affirmation of oneself is strength for a person to press on for better and more realization of fullness of life.

5.2.3. The Essential Goodness of Human Being to Do Good: With our assertion on the primacy of identity over dignity, we see the essential goodness of human being to do good as we explicate it further.

5.2.3.1. ***Karma reflects identity*:** The term *karma* has been understood as determining our human dignity, which causes us to look at *karma* as the source of the condition of all beings. In our cross cultural approach it is our conviction that *karma* is caused by our identity, who we are, not *karma* determining who we are. In this reversal understanding of the term *karma,* a person, who loses identity or whose identity is jeopardized, is stabilized to do good work.

5.2.3.2. ***Capacity to do good work*:** Being a human, everyone is capable to do good for he/she knows what is good and evil. Everyone, who possesses the consciousness of good, is worth to do good work not because of his/her dignity but because of who he/she is. If a person's action is considered unworthy it is a denial of his/her humanity. We, therefore, argue that it is wrong to seek dignity in the midst of denial of identity. We do not need to claim our worth to do good, rather we need to claim the worthiness of our action for we are worthy to do good. When action is denied, it is not because that action is not good, it is rather because the essential identity of the doer is denied to do good.

5.2.3.3 ***Freedom with responsibility*:** It is our assertion to emphasize freedom with responsibility. The Political, religious, social and economic status and dignities are not the essence of human identity. Human identity lies in the capacity and potential of becoming. The equality of everyone is not in relation to some object; such like God, but we are all distinctively equal to do good. However, it is not that those who do great works are better human

[310] James H. Cone, *God of the Oppressed* (New York: Seabury Press, 1975), p. 147.

being than those who do not. It is only that some people are not in a condition to do good because their freedom is denied; opportunity and responsibility are not given equally.

5.2.4. Values of Life in Self-Transcendence: It is very important to ask whether life is valuable. What are the values in it? As we are seeking the values of life, we are, here, dealing with two important values in order to realize the meaning and importance. Life is not worth living unless there is no value in it.

5.2.4.1. *The bond of love*: Panikkar explicates "Love is a nondualistic experience. Love is neither equality nor otherness, neither one nor two. Love requires differentiation without separation; it is a "going" toward "the other" that rebounds in a genuine "entering" into oneself by accepting the other within one's bosom."[311] Religion has been a dehumanizing force so long as fundamentalism and exclusivism leads to hatred and division among the people. Politics and society is evil so long as it leads to hierarchical structure dividing the community into various layers. All we need in such a context is to dialogue with mutual love and care, accepting each other in our differences.

5.2.4.2. *The forgiveness*: It is necessary to consider the importance of 'forgiveness' in life. Forgiveness is not the approval of wrong doings to the extent of negation of evil deeds. If forgiveness is negation of evil, it turns into a dehumanizing factor. If forgiveness is done with penalty alone, it will surely fall into a *karmic* bondage. Therefore, forgiveness is considering the acceptance of the wrong doings in such a manner that would lead us to mutual healing which may cost retribution or penalty. It is a mutual engagement in the process of realizing the worth of 'life in togetherness' till the realization of its worth to pay the cost of forgiveness. Forgiveness is neither to submit to authority nor to ignore evil. It requires self-transcendence to know the condition of others in order to realize our essential capacity of goodness, so that we can have a peaceful mutual interaction at the most.

Both 'love' and 'forgiveness' are based on human self-transcendency, which is to stand out of oneself (dignity) without removing one's identity which makes life worth living and beautiful.

---

[311] Panikkar, *The Fulness of Man ...*, p. 57.

Life is in fullness where there is mutual interaction through love and forgiveness.

5.3. Concluding Remarks:

To be human being is a challenge to seek the fullness of life that would be achieved in the process of becoming. It is our affirmation that everyone lives within certain cultural backgrounds where we experience meaning of life. It is our conviction that every culture is constitutive to the realization of the fullness of life. It is, therefore, to live is to dialogue to achieve life in fullness. Life is valuable and humanity is worth seeking for it is our conviction that every changes or transformation happen in life is not human becoming something else but only human in the becoming. It is through the corporate endeavor that we can realize the fullness of life and everyone is responsible and participants in the quest of humanity. Though seeking a life in community, we give value to every single life and assure that if a single life holds no value, then none is of worth. Life is meaningful when it is lived with self-transcending love and forgiveness with a hope to reach the goal of true humanity.

Bibliography

Dictionaries and Encyclopedia:

Burwick, Frederick. "Romanticism." In *The Encyclopedia of Christianity*. Edited by Erwin Fahlbusch, et al. Vol. 4. Grand Rapids, Michigan: Willian B. Eerdmans Publishing Company, 2005, pp. 741-752.

Crouter, Richard. "Enlightenment." In *The Cambridge Dictionary of Christian Theology*. Edited by Ian A. McFarland, et al. New York: Cambridge University Press, 2011, pp. 164-165.

Hage, Wolfgang. "Nestorians." In *The Encyclopedia of Christianity*. Edited by Erwin Fahlbusch, et al. Vol. 4. Grand Rapids, Michigan: Willian B. Eerdmans Publishing Company, 2005, pp. 721-723.

Hofmeister, Heimo. "Philosophical Anthropology." In *Encyclopedia of Christianity*. Edited by Erwin Fahlbusch, et al. Vol. I (A – B). Brill: William B. Eerdmans Publishing Company, 1999, pp. 75-76.

Levi, Anthony. "Enlightenment." In *Encyclopedia of Christian Theology*. Edited by Jean Yves Lacoste. Vol. 1. (A – F). New York, London: Routledge, 2005, p. 477-479.

Lyman, J. Rebecca. "Monophysites." In *The Encyclopedia of Christianity*. Edited by Erwin Fahlbusch, et al. Vol. 4. Grand Rapids, Michigan: Willian B. Eerdmans Publishing Company, 2005, pp. 637-638.

McFarland, Ian A. "Theological Anthropology." In *The Cambridge Dictionary of Christian Theology*. Edited by Ian A. McFarland, et al. New York: Cambridge University Press, 2011, pp. 501-504.

Richardson, Alan. "Demiurge." In *A Dictionary of Christian Theology.* Edited by Alan Richardson. Philadelphia: The Westminster Press, 1960, p. 90.

Ritschl, Dietrich. "Anthropology." In *Encyclopedia of Christianity.* Edited by Erwin Fahlbusch, et al. Vol. I (A – B). Brill: William B. Eerdmans Publishing Company, 1999, pp. 69-70.

Books:

Aquinas, Thomas. *The Summa Theologica.* Part I. QQ. LXXV – CII. Translated by Fathers of the English Dominican Province. London: Burns Oates and Washbourne Ltd., 1920.

Augustine. "On the Grace of Christ." In *Theological Anthropology.* Translated and edited by J. Patout Burns. Philadelphia: Fortress Press, 1981, pp. 61-108.

Barth, Karl. *Church Dogmatics.* Vol. III/2. Edinburgh: T & T Clark, 1960.

Barth, Karl. *The Theology of Schleiermacher.* Translated by Geoffrey W. Bromiley. Grand Rapids, Michigan: William B. Eerdmans Publishing Company, 1982.

Berkhof, L. *Systematic Theology.* Grand Rapids, Michigan: William B. Eerdmans Publishing Co., 1941.

Boff, Leonardo. *Jesus Christ Liberator.* Maryknoll, New York: Orbis Books, 1981.

Botman, H. Russel. "Covenantal Anthropology: Three Discourses of Human Dignity." In *God and Human Dignity.* Edited by R. Kendall Soulen and Linda Woodhead. Grand Rapids: William B. Eerdmans Publishing Company, 2006, pp. 72-86.

Boyd, Robin. *An Introduction to Indian Christian Theology.* Madras: The Christian Literature Society, 1969.

Brandt, Richard B. *The Philosophy of Schleiermacher.* New York and London: Harper & Brothers Publishers, 1941.

Brunner, Emil. *Man in Revolt.* Philadelphia: Westminster Press, 1939.

Cairns, David. *The Image of God in Man.* London: SCM Press Ltd., 1953.

Carney, Gerald T. "Christophany: The Christic Principle and Pluralism." In *The Intercultural Challenge of Raimon Panikkar* Edited by Joseph Prabhu. Maryknoll, New York: Orbis Books, 1996, pp. 131-144.

Christian, C. W. *Friedrich Schleiermacher: Makers of the Modern Theological Mind.* Texas: Word Books Publisher, 1979.

Clements, Keith W. *Friedrich Schleiermacher: Pioneer of Modern Theology.* London and San Francisco: Collins, 1987.

Cone, James H. *God of the Oppressed.* New York: Orbis Books, 1997.

Cousins, Ewert H. "Panikkar's Advaitic Trinitarianism." In *The Intercultural Challenge of Raimon Panikkar.* Edited by Joseph Prabhu. Maryknoll, New York: Orbis Books, 1996, pp. 199-130.

Crouter, Richard. "Introduction: *On Religion* in Its Cultural Mileu." In Friedrich Schleiermacher. *On Religion: Speeches to its Cultured Despisers.* Trans. and ed. by Richard Crouter. Cambridge Text in the History of Philosophy. London: Cambridge University Press, 1996, pp. xi-xxxix.

D'Sa SJ, Francis X. "The Notion of God." In *The Intercultural Challenge of Raimon Panikkar.* Edited by Joseph Prabhu. Maryknoll, New York: Orbis Books, 1996, pp. 25-45.

D'Sa SJ, Francis. "Forward: Fullness of "Man" or Fullness of "the Human"?" In Raimon Panikkar. *The Fulness of Man: A Christophany.* Translated by Alfred DiLascia. New York: Orbis Books and Delhi: ISPCK, 2006. pp. xvii-xxiii.

Feuerbach, Ludwig. *The Essence of Christianity.* Translated by George Eliot. New York: Harper and Brothers Publishers, 1957.

Friedrich, Carl J., ed. *The Philosophy of Kant.* New York: The Modern Library, 1949.

Gadamer, Hans Georg. *Truth and Method.* London: Sheed and Ward, 1988.

Gerrish, B. A. *A Prince of the Church: Schleiermacher and the Beginnings of Modern Theology.* Philadelphia: Fortress Press, 1984.

Grenz, Stanley J. and Roger E. Olson. *20th Century Theology.* Secunderabad: OM Authentic Books, 1992.

Kaufman, Gordon. *Systematic Theology: A Historical Perspective.* New York: Charles Scribner's Sons, 1968.

Kelsey, David H. *Eccentric Existence: A Theological Anthropology.* Vol. 1. Louisville, Kentucky: Westminster John Knox Press, 2009.

Komulainen, Jyri. *An Emerging Cosmotheandric Religion? Raimon Panikkar's Pluralitic Theology of Religions.* Helsinki: University of Helsinki, 2003.

Kuster, Volker. *The Many Faces of Jesus Christ.* Maryknoll, New York: Orbis Books, 2001.

Lanzetta, Beverly L. "The Mystical Basis of Panikkar's Thought." In *The Intercultural Challenge of Raimon Panikkar.* Edited by Joseph Prabhu. Maryknoll, New York: Orbis Books, 1996, pp. 91-105.

Livingston, James C., et al. *Modern Christian Thought.* Vol. II. The Twentieth Century. New Jersey: Prentice Hall, 2000.

Macquarrie, John. *In Search of Humanity.* London: SCM Pres Ltd; 1982.

Macquarrie, John. *Principles of Christian Theology.* New York: Charles Scribner's Sons, 1966.

Mays, James Luther. "The Self in the Psalms and the Image of God." In *God and Human Dignity.* Edited by R. Kendall Soulen and Linda Woodhead. Grand Rapids: William B. Eerdmans Publishing Company, 2006, pp. 27-43.

McGrath, Alister E. *Christian Theology: An Introduction.* Third Edition. Oxford: Blackwell Publishers Ltd., 2001.

Moltmann, Jurgen. *God in Creation.* London: SCM Press Ltd., 1985.

Moltmann, Jurgen. *Man: Christian Anthropology in the Conflicts of the Present.* Translated by John Sturdy. Minneapolis: Fortress Press, 1974.

Moltmann, Jurgen. *The Trinity and the Kingdom of God: The Doctrine of God.* London: SCM Press Ltd, 1981.

Niebuhr, Reinhold. *The Nature and Destiny of Man.* One Volume Edition. New York: Charles Scribner's Sons, 1949.

Niebuhr, Richard R. *Schleiermacher on Christ and Religion.* London: SCM Press Ltd, 1964.

Otto, Rudolf. "Introduction." In Friedrich Schleiermacher. *On Religion: Speeches to its Cultured Despisers.* Translated by John Oman. New York: Harper & Brothers, 1958, pp. vii-xx.

Panikkar, R. "Indian Theology: A Theological Mutation." In *Theologizing in India.* Edited by Amaladoss, T. K. John and G. Gispert-Sauch. Bangalore: Theologica Publications in India, 1981, p. 23-42.

Panikkar, R. *The Intrareligious Dialogue.* New York: Paulist Press, 1978.

Panikkar, Raimon. "Colligite Fragmenta: For an Integration of Reality." In *From Alienation to At-Oneness.* Edited by F. A. Eigo. Villanova, PA.: Villanova University Press, 1977, pp. 19-91.

Panikkar, Raimon. *A Dwelling Place for Wisdom.* Translated by Annemarie S. Kidder. Delhi: Motilal Banarsidass, 1993.

Panikkar, Raimon. *The Fulness of Man: A Christophany.* Translated by Alfred DiLascia. New York: Orbis Books and Delhi: ISPCK, 2006.

Panikkar, Raimond. "The Theological Challenge of the 21st Century: The Harmony Among Religions." In *Indian Theology Seeking New Horizons.* Edited by Kuncheria Pathil and Mathew Paikada. Mumbai: St. Pauls, 2007, pp. 132-137.

Panikkar, Raimundo. *The Silence of God: The Answer of the Buddha.* Translated by Robert R. Barr. Maryknoll, New York: Orbis Books, 1989.

Panikkar, Raimundo. *The Unknown Christ of Hinduism.* Revised and enlarged edition. Bangalore: ATC, 1982.

Panikkar, Raimundo. *Worship and Secular Man.* London: Darton, Longman and Todd Ltd., 1973.

Panikkar, Raymond. *Myth Faith and Hermeneutics: Cross Cultural Studies.* New York: Paulist Press, 1979.

Panikkar, Raymond. *The Trinity and World Religions.* Madras: CLS, 1970.

Pannenberg, Wolfhart. *Anthropology in Theological Perspective.* Edinburgh: T & T Clark Ltd, 1985.

Parappally, Jacob. *Emerging Trends in Indian Christology.* Bangalore: IIS Publications, 1995.

Pathil, Kuncheria and Mathew Paikada, eds. *Indian Theology Seeking New Horizons.* Mumbai: St. Pauls, 2007.

Pathil, Kuncheria. *Trends in Indian Theology.* Bangalore, India: Asian Trading Corporation, 2005.

Pauck, Wilhelm. "Schleiermacher's Conception of History and Church History." In *Schleiermacher as Contemporary.* Edited by Robert W. Funk. New York: Herder and Herder, 1970, pp. 41-47.

Pelagius. "Letter to Demetrias." In *Theological Anthropology.* Translated and edited by J. Patout Burns. Philadelphia: Fortress Press, 1981, pp. 39-45.

Peters, Ted. *God The World's Future.* Minneapolis: Fortress Press, 2000.

Prabhu, Joseph. "Lost in Translation," in *The Intercultural Challenge of Raimon Panikkar.* Edited by Joseph Prabhu. Maryknoll, New York: Orbis Books, 1996, p. 1-21.

Redeker, Martin. *Schleiermacher: Life and Thought.* Translated by John Wallhausser. Philadelphia: Fortress Press, 1973.

Ries, Julien. "Presentation: Anthropologlical perspectives for the third mellienium." In Raimon Panikkar. *The Fulness of Man: A Christophany.* Translated by Alfred DiLascia. New York: Orbis Books and Delhi: ISPCK, 2006, pp. xi-xvi.

Roberts, Alexander and James Donaldson, eds. *The Ante-Nicene Fathers.* Vol. 7. Grand Rapids: Eerdmans, 1971.

Robinson, John A. T. *The Human Face of God.* Philadelphia: Westminster Press, 1973.

Schleiermacher, Friedrich. *Brief Outline on the Study of Theology.* Richmond: John Knox Press, 1966.

Schleiermacher, Friedrich. *On Religion: Speeches to its Cultured Despisers.* Translated by John Oman. New York: Harper & Brothers, 1958.

Schleiermacher, Friedrich. *The Christian Faith.* Edited by H. R. Mackintosh and J. S. Stewart. Edinburgh: T & T Clark, 1928.

Sobrino, Jon. *Christology at the Crossroads.* London: SCM Press Ltd, 1978.

Sobrino, Jon. *Jesus in Latin America.* Maryknoll, New York: Orbis Books, 1987.

Sobrino, Jon. *Jesus the Liberator.* Maryknoll, New York: Orbis Books, 2004.

Soulen, R. Kendall and Linda Woodhead. "Introduction: Contextualizing Human Dignity." In *God and Human Dignity.* Edited by R. Kendall Soulen and Linda Woodhead. Grand Rapids: William B. Eerdmans Publishing Company, 2006, pp. 1-24.

Spiegler, Gerhard. "Theological Tensions in Schleiermacher's *Dialectic.*" In *Schleiermacher as Contemporary.* Edited by Robert W. Funk. New York: Herder and Herder, 1970, pp. 13-40.

Sykes, Stephen. *Friedrich Schleiermacher.* Atlanta: John Knox Press, 1971.

Tertullian. *Treatise on the Resurrection.* With text, ed. and trans. by Ernest Evans. London: SPCK, 1960.

Thangaraj, M. Thomas. *The Crucified Guru.* Nashville: Abingdon Press, 1994.

Thangasamy. D. A. *The Theology of Chenchiah with Selections from His Writings.* Bangalore: CISRS, 1966.

Theophilus of Antioch. *Ad Autolycum.* Text and trans. by Robert M. Grant. Oxford: Clarendon, 1970.

Thomas, M. M. and P. T. Thomas. *Towards Indian Christian Theology.* Thiruvalla: The New Day Publications of India, 1992.

Thomas, M. M. *Salvation and Humanisation.* Madras: Christian Literature Society, 1971.

Tillich, Paul. *Systematic Theology.* Vol. I. London: NISBET & Co., Ltd., 1953.

Wyman, Jr., Walter E. "Sin and Redemption." In *The Cambridge Companion to Friedrich Schleiermacher.* Edited by Jacqueline Marina. New York: Cambridge University Press, 2005, pp. 129-150.

Articles:

Cameron, Charles. "An Introduction to 'Theological Anthropology'." *Evangel.* 23.2. Summer, 2005, pp. 53-61.

Panikkar, R. "The Silence of the Word: Non-dualistic Polarities." In *Cross Currents.* 24. No. 2-3. Sum-Fall, 1974, pp. 154-171.

Panikkar, Raimond. "The Cosmotheandric Intuition." *Jeevadhara.* 14. January, 1984, pp. 27-35.

Panikkar, Raimundo. "The Myth of Pluralism: The Tower of Babel – A meditation on Non-violence." In *Cross Currents.* 29. no 2. Sum, 1979, pp. 197-230.

Webliography:

"Christian Perspectives on Theological Anthropology." http://www.oikoumene.org/fileadmin/files/wcc-main/documents/p2/FO2005, 199, en.pdf. p. 1. Accessed on 5th October, 2012.